H♥ARTFELT

A MEMOIR OF POLITICAL INTRIGUE, PASSION AND PERSEVERANCE

Richard W. Blide, M.D.

to todd & Patty,
you have great parents + good
friends of ours.

Dick Blide 1/29/13

ISBN-13: 978-0-9788580-3-2

Library of Congress Control Number: 2008927537

1. Memoir–Richard W. Blide 2. Health Care. 3. Small-town Politics.

Cover design by Patti Blide. Cover photo of Pagosa Springs, Colorado, by Jeff Laydon, Pagosa Springs.

www.cedarknollbooks.com

Distributed by Franklin, Beedle & Associates, www.fbeedle.com

Manufactured in the United States of America.

CEDAR KNOLL
BOOKS

Blide takes a ride. And, what a ride it was. But, it was a ride well worth the time, the energy, the frustration—for Dick Blide's involvement in what can only be described as a tragicomedy of the highest order resulted in a great gift to the community in which he once lived, labored, suffered and, eventually, triumphed. This story, while an account of what happened in a small Colorado mountain community, also stands as an example of what occurs anywhere, at any level, when hubris and dishonesty come to the fore in politics and management. And of what can happen when determined, well-intentioned and honest people refuse to accept that fact and work with like-minded comrades to serve the common good.

- Karl Isgard, Editor, *Pagosa Springs Sun*, Pagosa Springs, Colorado

"It's not my job."
We hear this statement daily and each of us thinks it when we are faced with an almost insurmountable and very unpleasant task. Most people would (and did) back off the disaster that was destroying our local healthcare system. It would have been so easy for Dick Blide to say that he had already done his deeds for mankind and that he was now in Colorado to enjoy "Paradise" and the fruits of a career as a recently-retired physician. But Dick has always done the unusual. He took a complex and almost unsolvable problem, withstood vitriolic verbal assaults, never let up despite serious health problems, continued to speak the truth while enduring constant vilification and all in an almost Churchillian stance to help his fellow man. The outcome speaks for itself: a brand new hospital and a first-rate healthcare system. But the most important outcome for me was that I found a kindred soul and a true lifelong friend.

- James L. Knoll, M.D., Retired Chairman, Department of
  Psychiatry, Presbyterian Hospital of Dallas; Professor of
  Psychiatry, University of Texas Southwestern Medical School
  of Dallas

I found the entire story to be riveting. I was absolutely absorbed by this unique look at small town politics as seen from an insider, and a very perceptive, articulate insider. It is so clear, and so well organized. I was led step by step through the story with my interest growing as each new twist and turn unfolded.

- Rich Weaver, Ph.D., Playwright, Professor Emeritus and Chair of
  the Department of Theatre and Dance, Texas Tech University

Patience and perseverance have a magical effect before which difficulties disappear and obstacles vanish.

- John Q. Adams

This book is dedicated to the directors
of the board and committee members
of the Upper San Juan Health Service District
of Pagosa Springs, Colorado

ACKNOWLEDGEMENTS

My wife Patti was a bedrock of support throughout the ordeal of the events in this story. Her charisma has always been there to brighten my day and to diminish what seemed to me to be insurmountable problems. Her literary background helped immensely in the writing of this story.

Dr. Jim Knoll's critique and support was instrumental in my weathering the time I spent on the USJHSD board. His original and brilliant vision, "The Six-Point Plan," and then his leadership served as the basis for the successes in this story.

My editor, Mason Smith, provided thoughtful and insightful editing and a hundred and one other suggestions which added to the quality of this book. His efforts are greatly appreciated.

Thanks to Jeff Laydon for providing the cover evening photo of Pagosa Springs and the photo of the Pagosa Mountain Hospital.

I appreciate the photographs taken by Maria Kolvin and Norm Vance.

CONTENTS

Book I: MAELSTROM

Book II: A NEW DAY

Pagosa Peak. Photo: Maria Kolvin.

PREFACE

A beautiful resort town in southwest Colorado is the scene of a Machiavellian drama being played out in a circus-like atmosphere. The local citizenry is slowly awakening to a catastrophe developing within their midst. Health care is being held hostage by a group more concerned with self-interest and self-preservation than in the medical needs of the community.

Naively, a retired physician enters this fray expecting that his advice will be sought because of his past experience and expertise in health care. As it turns out, he has figuratively stepped in front of a roaring train because he will not toe-the-line with the medical board he has joined. He is ostracized and vilified. A story is fabricated in an attempt to remove him from office resulting in his having to go to court to defend himself. So, this tale is born, that of political intrigue and the passion and perseverance that it wrought. Character, reputation and what is felt to be right are all called into question and are at stake.

This story is a microcosm of life and health care in rural America; a tale worth telling, if for no other reason, than the hard lessons learned. It exposes the problems that can occur in civic organizations; how they can destroy and how they can be corrected and avoided. Through this story, we see the risks and rewards of volunteer work. With planning and discipline, and yes, trial and error too, a battle ensues that defines the character of this small mountain town.

This factual memoir is abundantly documented from a personal journal, newspaper archives, government sources, recordings of board meetings, personal conversations and from literally hundreds of saved emails from various sources. The time period of this story is 2003 through 2005 with an epilogue updating activities through 2008.

The names of some characters in this story have been changed to assure anonymity.

CHAPTER 1

MAELSTROM

"Oh, my God," I hear myself say.

Here in our new hometown of Pagosa Springs, Colorado, I am attending a meeting of the local Health Service District Board. Citizens in the audience are shouting angrily at the board members. The chairman of the board is hurling back surly retorts. Board members at the fold-up tables up front sit motionless, puppet-like. A burly policeman is escorting one of the agitated audience toward the exit at the chairman's behest. I muse that instead of a sedate town meeting I must be in the midst of a Saturday night bar room brawl.

Later I read the apt words of a reporter for the local newspaper describing these meetings as "...a circus without the benefit of cotton candy or elephants."[1]

Seeking a meaningful new life just six months before, I had thrust myself into the midst of this maelstrom not knowing what to anticipate but certainly not expecting the theatrics that were now swirling about me.

After 44 years of an urban life and medical practice, my wife Patti and I had retired and moved to this small mountain resort town in Colorado. We had always relished the outdoor life from afar and had skied and hiked when we could squeeze it into our busy work schedules. Now that it was at our doorstep, we had immediately immersed ourselves into this new environment, joining the local outdoor clubs and participating in their activities. Personally, I had been looking forward to this new lifestyle all my working life.

I had expected retirement from my years of practicing medicine to be an emotionally rewarding experience. I realized that there would no longer be the challenge or the gratification that comes from solving patient problems, but instead that I would finally have the time to do all those things that had been put off until retirement. I had always thought that the latter would outweigh the former. I would finally be able to relax after decades of work and enjoy the fruits of my labor. Alas, rather than an emotional high, retirement for me had turned out to be a letdown. I had enjoyed my work; it was enlivening. The rewards in retirement so far did not measure up to this level. Realization was setting in; I needed more purpose in my life, a feeling that had been lost in retirement. So I began seeking something that could replace the stimulation I had experienced in my medical practice, hence, my quiet appearance at this "circus without the benefit of cotton candy or elephants."

It was now the fall of 2002. I was becoming concerned by a health care controversy that was erupting in our community. From articles in the local newspaper, particularly in the letters-to-the-editor section, it was clear that considerable anger and animosity were building within the community toward the Health Service District. Perhaps, with my experience in health care, I might be able to help in solving this health care dilemma and simultaneously assuage my need for a more purposeful fulfillment in life.

And so, with little more thought, I entered into one of those unexpected lifetime experiences that occasionally come one's way; daunting, challenging, perhaps even rewarding. I had no idea of the emotional swings I would experience or of the challenges my character and reputation were to face.

In January 2003 I attended a board meeting of the Upper San Juan Health Service District (USJHSD). I was surprised that by the time the meeting started the room was packed, including standees at the back of the room. I thought it remarkable that a small town of 1500 people could garner a standing-room-only crowd. There were loud murmurings all around me. I sensed an air of excitement as well as a tinge of smoldering anger in the crowd. The room itself was old fashioned, small and plain with windows on two sides. Two long fold-up tables sat end-to-end across the front of the room with armchairs behind them facing the audience for the board members. Fold-up chairs with faded plastic seats were provided for the audience. A secretary sat to one side ready to transcribe the proceedings once they started.

While waiting for the meeting to begin, I turned to a couple seated beside me who appeared to be about my age; he graying and bespectacled, both giving the impression of being comfortable in their later years. They returned my smile and we began conversing. This was the first board meeting for Don and Elaine too, and they had been prompted to attend for my same reason. They had been upset by the health care controversy that they had been reading about in our local weekly paper. They wondered, as did I, what could be going on to cause such a furor in this small town.

The meeting began by going over the minutes of the previous meeting and then reviewing the finances of the month just passed. It was mentioned that, whereas the finances had been in atrocious shape at the beginning of last year, they were now vastly improved. This was attributed, in part, to an increase in the mil levy tax on property, but also to better management by the administration.

The subsequent agenda included a few minor matters of little consequence. The meeting was then opened to the public for general comments and questions. Without introduction, a short, trim man jumped up in the back and in a loud voice began castigating the board and particularly the administration. I twisted around to see him as did most of the crowd.

"Why is the district manager so hard on the employees? She's been here just a year and already half the employees have either been fired or quit. They can't take the pressure anymore. Can't the board see what's going on here? If you can't do your job, you should resign. You can all be recalled. Why don't you do something about it?"

This frustrated man then went on to mention that a number of employees had been fired apparently for no reason other than that they had voiced some minor disagreement with the district's policies. He accused the district manager of being personally vindictive against the employees. He called for her resignation. Another man yelled out, "You tell 'em, Toby." Several other audience members rose and voiced similar complaints almost as vociferously as had Toby. There was anger in their voices and more than a murmur of support from the crowd. I sensed an actual air of hostility. I leaned toward the couple beside me and said to Don in a low voice, "I can see why a new manager would want to weed out disgruntled employees but letting half the workers go seems excessive." He nodded in agreement.

Finally, a board member stood up. She said that she supported the employees and that she could no longer tolerate either the harsh treatment of the workers by the district manager or the tolerance of the board for these actions. "I have never served on a board that operates . . . or doesn't operate at all like this board."

She stated, further more, that the board members, including herself, had broken the state's "open meeting laws" by communicating with each other by email, not realizing that board directors may discuss company business with no more than one other director at a time outside an official board meeting, including email. For these reasons she was resigning her position as a director on the board. She called for the resignation of the district manager and felt that the entire board should be recalled by petition of the citizenry, a procedure whereby elected officials can be removed from office. Forthwith, she strode out to sit with the audience. Several people in the audience yelled out, "Don't do it, Kay."[2] I later learned that she was the fire chief's wife. I did wonder if there weren't others on the board that might feel the same way as she but weren't speaking out or taking action for whatever reasons.

Then a member of the audience arose and in a more conciliatory tone suggested that the district hire a mediator to arbitrate the differences between the employees, the administration, and the board. Several board members finally spoke up to support this suggestion. I noticed a heavy-set woman at the head of the table seemingly just bridling to speak. I concluded that she must be the district manager (DM).

"This would cost the district thousands of dollars," she said. "We don't have that kind of money." Clearly she was not in favor of such a move. This determined, middle-aged woman with her '50's bouffant hairdo spoke authoritatively and with a condescending smile. I later learned that her name was Eve Hegarty, and she was indeed the DM. She gave the appearance of great confidence, as if she were a force to be reckoned with.

An audible wave of frustration swept through the audience. Then a young woman stood up, appearing visibly shaken. In a voice quivering with emotion, she stated that she worked at the clinic and could no longer take the harassment or the pressure being placed on her by the DM. Therefore, she was quitting her job. Immediately, another woman jumped up. She, too, was quitting her job at the clinic, voicing the same concerns. This brought a loud clamor of support from the audience and an outpouring of, "No, don't quit." I was impressed by the animation in the crowd. They responded as one, like a tiger protecting its brood or ready to jump on its prey at the first sign of weakness. It seemed evident by the reticence of the board to speak that the DM was calling the shots. I was surprised to see the subservience of the board to this administrator. It should have been just the opposite, or at least a more even balance of power. I wondered how such a bizarre situation could develop in this seemingly quiet, sleepy mountain town.

Even though I was just a first-time observer, I was becoming incensed by the action, or rather inaction, on the part of the board. Mediation certainly seemed the appropriate first step to resolve this controversy between the employees and the administration. I have always been a quiet, mild-mannered person but on occasion I do get riled up. On a sudden impulse I jumped up and heard myself say, "I'll be happy to pay the expense of bringing in a mediator if the administration doesn't feel they can afford it." There were murmurs of surprise and support from the audience, as well as many craning necks looking to glimpse this stranger in their midst. The DM looked irritated, even embarrassed. After a moment's pause, she said in a belittling tone, "I think we might be able to find the money to hire a mediator."

It looked like it didn't take much bucking to get her to back down. On the other hand, she had a pretty flimsy excuse for not hiring a mediator, particularly when it appeared that a crisis situation was developing, and had they not just minutes before stated that their finances were in good shape? Thereafter, the board finally became involved and discussed where to find a mediator. Eventually they chose a woman experienced in mediation from Durango, a larger town to the west.

As the meeting broke up, I again conversed with my new friends, Don and Elaine, and told them that I might run for the just vacated board seat. With my medical background and being a retired physician with time on his hands, I felt that I could help move the health district in the right direction. Surprisingly, Don said that with his administrative background he, too, might run for this seat. He was a retired physicist from Sandia Labs in Albuquerque. I wondered if there would be others as interested in volunteering for what looked like an undesirable seat, at least on this board.

I left the meeting heartened by the feeling that, at least in a small way, my outburst may have helped move the health district in the right direction.

On returning home, I related to my wife, Patti, the events of the evening. I said I was thinking of applying for the just vacated board seat. She was very supportive, being aware of the void that I had felt since retiring from medical practice. However, she wondered if getting involved in such a volatile situation wouldn't be too stressful. In our retirement we both had been looking for a simpler, more peaceful lifestyle. We had accomplished that goal in that we now had a beautiful mountain home and we were enjoying hiking and skiing with our friends year-round. Still, after my many years in medical practice, I felt the need for a more purpose-driven life.

I have always admired people who give of their time and talents for volunteer work. I had thought that this was always purely altruistic, not thinking that there might be some reward in return. Both Patti and I had enjoyed our work of providing services for people, she as a teacher and I as a physician. We had been abundantly rewarded outside of our remuneration, knowing when we had accomplished a job well-done, including Patti's well-deserved selection as "Teacher of the Year" in Richardson, Texas. I suspected that volunteer work might be even more rewarding when it was completely altruistic, giving without expecting any monetary return. I decided to go ahead and apply for the board position.

In the interim month, before the next board meeting, several other persons submitted their names for the vacated board position: Dr. Jim Knoll, J.R. Ford, Walter Perkins and new friend Don Lundergan, who had been sitting next to me. I knew Dr. Jim Knoll was a psychiatrist who had just returned from a six-month *locum tenens* (temporary practice of medicine) in New Zealand. I had heard that J.R. Ford was a prominent businessman in town. I knew nothing of Walter Perkins but I had heard that he was supported by the DM and some of the board members.

J. R. Ford and Dr. Jim Knoll

The mediator from Durango was soon hired to assess the employee/employer controversy. She began immediately by interviewing the employees of the Dr. Mary Fisher Medical Center (clinic) and the Emergency Medical Service (EMS) as well as the administrative staff, some board members, and even some of the concerned citizenry. Within the month, she had already submitted a preliminary report. I hadn't seen the report but I was impressed by the swiftness of her initial efforts.

The next month's board meeting in February produced another packed house. Again, one could sense the restlessness in the crowd. After the preliminary reports, Eve, the DM, stated that a mediator had been hired for an initial evaluation of the employee controversy. The mediator had conducted initial interviews and had submitted her report, copies of which were distributed to the audience. Her report stated that a 'culture of conflict' existed between the employees and the administration, and she felt this needed immediate attention. She suggested mediating these differences by forming small groups of "healing circles" consisting of both employees and administrative staff. In addition, she felt that there were irreconcilable differences between the board chairman and the employees, so she recommended that the chairman resign. Lastly, a contract was submitted to cover the continuing work to be done. Several audience members took the floor and applauded the mediator's report. One of them commented, "By George, I think she's got it."[3]

At this point board chairman Dick Babillis, an older, gray-haired, fit-looking gentleman, took the floor. He said that in view of the mediator's recommendation, and after careful consideration, he realized that it was time for a change in leadership. "I believe tonight we are at a crossroads. An opportunity now exists to move into the future by building new relationships and creating a new vision."[4]

In an attempt to speed up the process, he said he was stepping down as board chairman. There were murmurs of approval from the audience. I thought it odd that the mediator would make this, a major recommendation, after just a preliminary review of the situation. Just as strange was the chairman's immediate acceptance of this recommendation. Perhaps he was happy to get out of what he saw as a no-win situation for himself.

I felt ambivalent about the now-former chairman. I hadn't seen him do anything wrong, nor had he said anything in particular to aggravate the employees at the two meetings I had attended. On the other hand, he hadn't done anything to alleviate this tenuous situation at the last board meeting or apparently before, either. I presumed that the lack of action on his and the Board's part spoke volumes by itself. The problem was so obvious that I thought that he and the DM, between the two of them, should have been able to find a resolution for the employee dilemma. However, it looked like the DM was calling all the shots. It was my understanding that boards usually look to the chairman to lead. Obviously this had not happened in this situation, nor had anyone else on the board stepped in to fill the void. I did wonder who would be the new board chairman. No one presently on the board seemed up to the task.

The board then discussed the contract submitted by the mediator. One member thought the price was too high. Another wondered if they couldn't find a local person to do the job and then mentioned several names. No one gave any indication as to why the Durango mediator might not be the best person other than the cost. Finally, and frustratingly, the board tabled approving the contract of the mediator from Durango to the next meeting. This seemed to be an obvious delaying tactic, likely at the behest of the DM.

As the meeting broke up, I heard many disgruntled comments around me, the essence being that these were the same old tactics that they had seen previously. To me, it seemed odd the way the course of events had transpired in just the two Board sessions I had attended. I was perplexed by the intransigence of the administration and the Board to address the problem with their employees. At this time I couldn't imagine why this problem should have occurred, particularly after it appeared that the District had weathered a worse situation, a financial crisis, and had come through in good shape.

As we shall see, other important events subsequently occurred that obscured hiring a mediator. The subject died an ignominious death, never again to be broached. The employee situation remained unresolved.

I had met Dr. Jim Knoll, one of the other candidates for a board position, briefly several years before on a cross country ski trip. Now seeing him in the audience I gravitated in his direction. Tall, with a short graying beard and a self-assured presence, he looked to be the quintessential, archetypical psychiatrist. A crinkle about his eyes as he smiled suggested that he was also a kind, friendly person. He recognized me, too. We shook hands. It is interesting how you can meet someone and in a blink know that you are "simpatico" with them for reasons not clear at the time.

We discussed the meeting that had just ended and concurred that both the administration and board had major problems that seemed beyond their capacity to solve. Even at this early stage of our knowledge, we agreed that the major problem appeared to revolve around the district manager and that the board seemed impotent to take control of the situation. The resignation of the chairman was perplexing. Neither of us knew board chair Babillis, so at this time we had no idea what his influence had been on the district in the past or what impact his resignation might have on the future of the district. Later, in retrospect, this was a crucial decision that would have a far-reaching effect on health care in our town for some time to come.

I told Jim Knoll that I had decided to run for a board seat and he said that he had been thinking of doing the same. We decided to meet for lunch to talk about what we might do should we both be elected to the board considering that there were two board seats now vacant.

CHAPTER 2

BAPTISM

We were notified that a special board meeting would be held to interview applicants for the two recently-vacated board positions. Unfortunately, I would be in Los Angeles at the time, visiting with family. The DM indicated that they would call me during the meeting for the interview. The tele-conference call turned out to be a non-event, primarily queries about my past medical experience and how I might act as a new board member. What could I say? I replied that I would follow a policy that would be in the best interests of the community, without being more specific and without making any reference to the district's current problems.

I had no idea how the other interviews had gone. Presumably Jim Knoll, Walter Perkins and J.R. Ford had been interviewed and that Don Lundergan, the man who had sat next to at the first meeting, had been contacted as well.

COUNTERPOINT

To present a more balanced view I am giving a theoretical voice to what will become the opposition of the two sparring parties in this memoir. This is a conversation that DM Eve and board applicant Walter Perkins might have had prior to the March board meeting. It is obvious that these parties knew each other beforehand:

Eve pondering, "Wally, since Dick resigned as chairman we need to replace him with someone we can trust. Neither Betty nor Martha has any interest in being chairman. You and I think alike and

I believe we both agree on the future direction of the district. So, I'm asking you to be board chairman. We have enough votes to get you elected to the board and to make you chairman, too."

"Eve, I'll do it. I can finish Dick's term. It is just a little more than a year. I think we will make a good team. Between the two of us we can make things happen our way. We need to choose a second board member, Eve, someone we can get along with and who might join our team. It needs to be someone the other side can accept, too. We have never had a doctor on the board, and we need to appease the crowd and quiet them down. We have two docs, Jim Knoll and Dick Blide. I think the crowd would be happy with either of them on the board. Jim's a psychiatrist. He's head of PACK, the group that is involved in local politics. He is too opinionated for me. He would be trouble from the get-go. That leaves Blide. He's quiet and soft-spoken. I don't think he would give us trouble. I think I can handle him."

"It sounds good to me, Wally. I will check with the others. I am sure I can obtain the votes to get you elected, and Dick, too."

The March board meeting produced a large and restless crowd, perhaps more so because of the impending election of new board members. After the obligatory agenda items were concluded, the temporary chairman, sitting in for the just retired board chairman, moved on to the selection of the new directors. There were now 6 candidates: Dr. Jim Knoll, Don Lundergan, Walter Perkins, J.R. Ford and myself plus another person whom no one seemed to know.

The election process had each of the five current board members write the two names of those they favored on a slip of paper and hand it to the secretary, who would tally the results. Simply, the two highest vote-getters would be the new board members. I was sitting with Jim Knoll as we watched the proceedings. Because we appeared to think alike, I felt that whatever the result, we would become good friends.

Board secretary Martha arose and gave the results. Walter had garnered the most votes, I was second, and Jim third. Walter and I were immediately asked to come forward to take the oath of office. We then took seats with the other board members. Awkwardness and self-consciousness described my initial feelings. After all, I was now sitting with those for whom I had previously felt some disdain. The audience had shown no reaction whatever throughout the election proceedings, as if this had been a non-event. However, I did feel proud that I had made this move and had been successful.

The next item of business was to elect a new chairman of the board. Betty Moore, who appeared to be the oldest board member, immediately nominated Wally Perkins. A very audible groan wafted toward us from the audience. Not one voice, but numerous utterances, melded together. This seemed an ominous sign. What had Walter done in the past to engender this reaction?

I noted, too, that apparently Walter was "Wally" to everyone, a friendlier moniker which time would show was somewhat ironic. In fact, Wally himself said he preferred to be called Walter.

No further names were nominated and there was no discussion, as if his selection were foreordained. It seemed odd that a new board member without previous experience would be chosen to head the board. Surely one of the experienced board members should have realized the seriousness of the situation and stepped forward in this time of need. Presumably, even in this dire circumstance, no one was willing to take the position. Perhaps Eve had handpicked Wally to be chairman. Why else would he have been the only nominee for the position? Still, choosing a person without experience appeared to be the poorest of choices. Since I knew no one on the board, I was hardly in a position to question this decision or to make another nomination. So, I remained silent.

The motion was made and passed; Wally became the new chairman of the board.

Wally, a middle-aged, rather portly individual, exuded an air of confidence as he pounded his gavel loudly, signifying the beginning of his regime with a take-charge attitudee

Next on the agenda was the health district's public clinic, The Dr. Mary Fisher Medical Center. I had heard a rumor that the entire clinic staff had resigned including the physicians. Eve now stated, matter-of-factly, that irreconcilable differences had developed between the administration and the clinic; that the entire clinic staff, including the physicians, had resigned; and that she had accepted their resignations. She paused, as if expecting a reaction. A loud groan escaped from the audience. Unbelievably, not one of the board members made a comment. This matter must have been discussed before the meeting by the other directors and a decision made to accept the resignations without taking any action. How else could one explain their silence? It was beyond my comprehension that the board wouldn't consider talking to the clinic staff directly, particularly to the physicians, to get a clear picture as to why such a dire circumstance had occurred. Why could there not be some effort at reconciliation? As I voiced this concern, Wally took it upon himself to say that this situation had been developing for some time and that this inevitable outcome had been expected. Though his explanation was more elaborate than Eve's, it lacked any details as to why this had occurred. Looking up, I became aware of Eve shooting me a withering stare. It was becoming apparent that my original sense—that a lot went on outside these meetings—was correct, and that Wally was well aware of what had transpired before he took office. I looked at the other board members for support, and although some of them looked uncomfortable, no one said anything to clarify the picture or give support to the clinic staff. My thought then was that I had better get more information on this situation before saying anything further, so I shut up. Finally, Wally stated that a new clinic would be formed and any of the just-resigned staff were welcome to join them. This seemed pretty ironic, coming right after it was made clear that no attempt was going to be made to keep any of the clinic staff. I presumed it was just an attempt to mollify the crowd.

The audience was incensed by the clinic staff resignations and the board's lack of action. Many in the audience began angrily voicing their concerns. I knew that the clinic staff, including the physicians, were the care-givers as well as long-time friends of many in the audience. It must have been a catastrophic event for the entire clinic staff to have taken this action. This was a major event and not one to be laid easily to rest.

The board took this matter much as it had taken previous criticism. From their placidity, it could have been a non-event for all the reaction they showed. I saw that I needed to get more information regarding the board members, as well as the clinic situation, to better understand why they were so cowed. . . if that were actually the situation. Perhaps they were in agreement with the District manager for some unfathomable reason. The new board chairman appeared to support the DM. Perhaps he had been chosen for this position as a foil for the district manager. I also got the impression that one of the board members, Betty Moore, was joined-at-the-hip, so to speak, with these two, and I was beginning to suspect that there were others on the board that blindly supported the DM as well. It wouldn't be the first time that a management had stacked a board to do their bidding leaving me to wonder how I fit into this framework. This was my first meeting, and already I was having second thoughts about having made the choice to join this board. Why had I received votes second only to Wally? Had I been chosen for my medical acumen, or was I chosen because I looked to be the most easily manipulated?

I am introspective. It is my nature to wonder why things happen the way they do. Often I do not get an answer right away, but I have found that patience and perseverance, along with a good dose of pondering, will eventually produce an answer. I consider this to be one of the positive aspects of aging supported by experience.

The next item on the agenda was the establishment of several new committees. A Medical Advisory Committee (MAC) was established, and Dr. Jim Knoll was chosen to head this committee. I sensed that the administration might be trying to mollify the medical community by involving some physicians, be it only retired physicians, after the loss of their public clinic; first me and now Jim. Certainly it was a smart move on their part. The MAC committee was to include myself as the board representative. Jim would subsequently add to the committee the practicing physicians in town: Dr. Jim Pruitt's family medicine group and the just-recently resigned physicians, Drs. Mark Wienphal and Bob Brown. I had heard that Dr. Pruitt had been treated poorly by the district administration in the past. It was as if the district felt threatened by the physicians. This may not be an unusual circumstance when one is in power and knows that those more expert than you are looking over your shoulder. Again, one had to wonder whether this committee was being established as a "sop" to the physicians and community, or was it a true effort to heal the wounds of the past. Not wanting to feel we were entering an exercise in futility, we had to presume it was the latter.

Next, the board established a Citizen's Advisory Committee to be headed by Laura Mitchell a local, concerned citizen. I volunteered to be on this committee as well as the already existing Grants Committee, as I had experience in writing grants from my academic medical days.

The board meeting was then opened for comments and queries from the audience. Emotions ran high and a lot of disgruntled remarks were made, all regarding the closing of the Dr. Mary Fisher Clinic. It was obvious that the election of two new board members and the establishment of new committees, including a Medical Advisory Committee, had not at all appeased the crowd.

Wally reminded the crowd to show respect for the board. Someone in the audience hollered back that the board should show some respect for the citizens.[5] Several individuals called for the resignation of the DM, and one citizen presented a petition with 700 names on it calling for the resignation of the DM. This had been collected in less than 24 hours by citizens in the community. I was quite impressed. On the other hand, several people stood up and defended the DM, the first time I had heard any support for her.

I talked to Jim after the meeting. He congratulated me on becoming a new board member but then added that he had actually received some congratulations, too, for not having been elected. He laughed as he explained that perhaps he would be more useful in an advisory capacity, as head of the MAC. It seemed that he was actually happier in losing than I was in winning, a prescient assessment at the time. And so the cards were dealt, on one side a seemingly crafty team and on the other side a team of still unknown quantity and quality.

After the meeting, Jim and I walked over to join the throng crowding around Dr. Mark Weinphal, the just-resigned medical director of the clinic. He was getting queries from all directions about their resignations. He appeared harried and gave hurried responses, trying to satisfy everyone's concerns. We were finally able to introduce ourselves. He said he knew of us and indicated he was glad to meet us. We expressed our concerns about why the clinic staff had resigned. He said their staff was having a meeting the following evening, and he invited us to attend. We could get all our questions answered at that time. There was no way we would miss it.

The Dr. Mary Fisher Medical Clinic

The public clinic, The Dr. Mary Fisher Medical Center, had been established seven years previously. It was housed in a beautiful new building which had been supported by both a civic bond issue and private donations. It competed with a private concern, Dr. Jim Pruitt's Family Medicine Clinic, which was housed in a quaint log building right next door to the public clinic. Together they constituted a budding medical complex.

The health service district was composed of two components: the public clinic that we have been discussing and the Emergency Medical Service (EMS), which was the ambulance unit of the district. A population of about 12,000 lay within the district, which covered one county and small portions of two other counties.

Next evening, Jim and I met with the just-resigned clinic staff, eight employees in all. Dr. Mark Weinphal, lithe and tall with a full head of wavy black hair framing rimless glasses, had boyish good looks that belied his age. He came over to welcome us and then introduced us to his staff. The other doc present was Dr. Bob Brown, another fit and handsome younger man who told us that he had worked half-time at the clinic and was working half-time as an emergency room (ER) doc in Trinidad, a town about 100 miles east of our town of Pagosa Springs.

We then met nurse practitioner Susan Kuhns, who had been with Dr. Mark since the clinic had opened. Attractive and trim, probably in her mid thirties, she, like many Pagosans, appeared to have been drawn to this area by the outdoor life. She was unhappy with the clinic closing and mentioned that their other nurse practitioner, Dan Keunig, had resigned just a few weeks earlier and had taken a position with Dr. Jim Pruitt's Family Medicine Clinic. Apparently seeing the writing on the wall, Dan had made his move in anticipation of the closure.

Dr. Mark began the meeting informally, letting everyone voice their concerns. No one said that quitting had been the wrong decision. It was apparent that they had met previously and had jointly come to the decision to resign en masse. However, I had the feeling that some thought that their desperate act might awaken the board, which would then come to their rescue. These individuals seemed sorely disappointed that this had not occurred. Some voiced concerns that they were their family's only bread-winner and now they didn't know what they would do for income. No one had an answer for this worry. At the time this was what bothered me the most. Were things so bad that the entire clinic staff had to resign with no plans for survival? Was this the action of one or two individuals at the helm who couldn't take the "crud" any longer and so brought the entire ship down? Perhaps it was more a retaliatory response to the DM's harassment that would later be regretted. I had no answer for these sad thoughts.

Appearing to feel safe here in the home of one of their staff, the employees began to speak freely. One individual said that the DM often made outrageous requests and then demanded to know why they had not been met. Also, she would play the game of trying to turn one employee against the other by making insinuating remarks. I asked if the DM had acted this way all along. Someone said she had held the position of district manager for a little over a year and, yes, earlier there had been some signs of this attitude toward the employees but in the last several months her posture toward them had decidedly worsened. This was in spite of their bending over backwards, trying to acquiesce to her demands. Dr. Mark supported this assessment, saying that they had not been able to figure out why she had this attitude toward them. It was as if she were making a concerted effort to get rid of all the current employees. They indicated that between their clinic and the EMS staff, more than half the employees had been fired or had quit because of what they considered abusive treatment. So, it appeared that the harassment wasn't aimed just at the clinic but also included the EMS. This made me wonder if the EMS employees might be considering an action as drastic as that taken by the clinic staff. Truly, this could be a train about to run off the track.

We asked Dr. Mark what sort of personal experience he had with the DM. It still wasn't clear to either Jim or me why things had become so bad as to precipitate this mass exodus. Mark indicated that he, as the clinic medical director, and the DM met weekly. At these times he could make no headway in resolving either the employee problems or his own. It was like swimming in molasses, he said, trying to get anything done. He felt stone-walled at every attempt to get things moving in the right direction. I asked if he thought this was purposeful or the result of ineptness. He felt it was a conscious effort, but he had no explanation as to why this was occurring. He reiterated that they had all made efforts to diffuse the situation by being hypersensitive to the DM's requests and demands, but to no avail.

When Dr. Mark had talked to Eve after the clinic staff resignations, she had agreed to keep him on until he found a place for his patients, whom he did not want to desert. Dr. Bob and nurse practitioner Susan were turning their patients over to Dr. Mark until they could make arrangements of their own. I assumed that Eve hoped to find some way to retain these patients in a new clinic as well. Dr. Mark indicated that Eve was already looking for *locum* (temporary physicians) to work in the clinic until she could hire new permanent docs.

After the meeting, Jim and I stopped at the Dairy Queen (DQ) to discuss the situation. This practice was to become a habit. We both had fond memories of Dairy Queens from our former days in Texas. My memories included stopping at DQs on traveling through small Texas and New Mexico towns on our family drives up to our Colorado vacation home. Then, too, there were the stories of Larry McMurtry and the DQ in Archer City, Texas which we had actually visited, meeting McMurtry himself, which added to the allure. Jim had visited many DQs on trips throughout the Southwest. His wife Ingrid, an ice cream connoisseur, loved all the concoctions made famous by the DQ. Pagosa had no Dairy Queen, so we simply used the DQ name with a wink and a smile wherever we met. My wife Patti thought that this was a "guy thing" and similar to secret handshakes that she recalled Boy Scouts shared, and at a higher level, Masonic secrets. To this day Jim and I still converse by email sent from our fictitious DQ's.

Both of us could find no explanation for the DM's actions other than that she wanted complete control of the clinic and the personnel, and the only way to do that was to start over from scratch. We both acknowledged that a new boss had the right to get rid of disgruntled employees and form one's own team, but this appeared to go far beyond that action. DM Eve appeared hell-bent on a 100 percent turnover in personnel. This was bad from the standpoint that a good company's experienced employees serve as the backbone of any enterprise, and a completely new team would take at least one or two years to gain the experience needed to duplicate what had existed before. Furthermore, in a small community it would be difficult to hire all new good people, especially new docs, once they became aware of the shenanigans that had just transpired. Had the DM considered these probabilities? If so, she must have felt that she could overcome any obstacle. I felt this showed inexperience and poor judgment. These were just some of the ponderings that we stored for future reference. Time would make clear whether the DM's actions had been a mistake.

I later wondered if there wasn't some policy in place to which the employees could appeal for support. There was an old personnel policy manual, which needed to be revised and updated, but any appeal now went to the administrative staff which was controlled by the district manager herself. Knowing it was useless to complain or appeal, the employees had taken the only way out they knew: quitting. I later learned that not only had the entire clinic staff resigned, but half the staff of the EMS had quit or been fired, as well, since the beginning of the year. This was a tragedy that was escalating with no end in sight.

CHAPTER 3

MOUNTAIN INTERLUDE

The district and its problems were rapidly becoming an obsession. I needed a break.

Days were growing longer as gray skies gave way to ever more sunshine. Patti and I were anxious to get out and go cross country skiing before we lost the good snow. These forays into the mountains were the most relaxing way we knew to get away from the humdrum and stresses of everyday living. Westfork, one of our favorite places to ski, was at the base of Wolfcreek Mountain. This was an easy, mostly level trail on an old mountain road that led to the Rainbow Trailhead, which was one of our favorite summer hikes. Downhill skiing had given way to cross country skiing these days due to degenerative arthritis in our knees, a result of the trauma of years of long distance running. So, this was now our main winter sport, where we could enjoy the stillness, serenity, and beauty of forests and mountains.

On this particular day we stopped at the Subway to stuff our backpacks with veggie subs for lunch. The days temperature, in the high 20s, was complemented by sunshine blinking off of every mound of snow. It was a perfect day for our outing.

On starting out we noticed that someone had laid down a new track in the snow, allowing us to move along at a pretty good clip through the trees. With Patti leading the way, I was having a hard time keeping up with her. My brain was trying to find an explanation for this difficulty. I had just waxed our skis that morning. Maybe I had waxed just her skis. I am not really that forgetful. Being a little older than Patti, I wondered if my age was finally catching up with me. I thought no more about it then, but just worked hard to keep up.

During these outings, we always brought along our chocolate lab, Ghirardelli (GR), who loved running back and forth on the trail, bounding through the deep snow effortlessly with deer-like leaps. Her energy appeared limitless. On occasion we would stop just to watch her joyfulness at play, not having a care in the world.

A little way out we saw in the distance a snowmobile coming toward us. As it got closer, we saw that it was pulling the piece of equipment that was laying down our ski track. We both stopped. The driver, a gray-haired, bearded man, got out and introduced himself as Norm, a person we would later get to know well as being integrally involved in the health care crisis. Leaning on his shiny black snowmobile and grinning ear to ear, he explained that he was retired, having formerly been in the advertising and marketing business and more recently in radio. He and a friend now took pleasure in voluntarily getting out and putting down cross country ski trails for themselves and others. We thanked him for his efforts and continued on our way.

Several miles out we came to a meadow with a small pond, mostly frozen, but open enough for GR to get a drink of water. We stopped for a rest and shared a bottle of water ourselves and tossed GR a few doggy biscuits. Here we could admire the mountains soaring above us, a sight that we never tired of viewing. Rested, we continued on the trail, back into the forest, enjoying the rhythm of skiing, the repetition of the forward thrust and then the restful glide with the only sound being the soft hissing of the skis on the snow.

A few miles further out we stopped for lunch at "our" log, which was now buried under a foot of pristine, sparkling snow. After taking off our skis and backpacks, we started digging out. GR helped too, pushing the snow away with her paws. I could not figure out her motivation. I wondered if she thought she was helping in some way.

We sat, munching our subs and drinking our bottled water while watching GR hungrily gobbling up her biscuits as soon as we tossed them on the snow. Soaking up the scenery, we were especially aware of the complete silence broken only by the occasional puff of snow falling from a tree branch and plopping on the snow below. We met no one and welcomed the complete isolation. When Patti worried out loud about running into a mountain lion, having read about a woman cyclist being attacked while riding in a California forest, I "pooh-poohed" the idea, assuring her that we were much more likely to run into a bear. She neither laughed nor even smiled at my comparison.

After lunch, we continued skiing out to the Rainbow Trailhead and then turned to retrace our trail, always a faster trip back, the track still being slick from our trip out.

With our beautiful snow day ending, we knew there was one more pleasure awaiting us back in town. Wolftrack's Coffee House promised us warmth and conversation with a skinny latte for Patti and a hazelnut soy steamer for me, and, of course, a few more doggy biscuits for Ghirardelli. It was still a bright, sunny day in Pagosa so we sat outside, basking in the sun and letting our endorphins wind down while we relaxed with the feeling one gets only after having had a good workout. Could life get any better than this?

CHAPTER 4

A NEW CLINIC?

The following week Jim and I again met for lunch at the DQ. Jim had talked to J.R., a businessman in town, the day before. J.R., in turn, had contacted Drs. Mark and Bob, as well as Susan, the nurse practitioner, and was proposing to start a new private clinic that would include the former docs and clinic employees. J.R. was developing a business plan to see if this would be financially viable. The docs would offer to lease the clinic building from the district. Depending on the outcome of a feasibility study, they were planning on submitting a proposal to the board at the next monthly meeting. We both felt that this was an excellent idea. It would keep the clinic staff together and patient care would be continued uninterrupted. The one worry, a big one, was that district manager Eve might have plans of her own.

The board of directors of the USJHSD at this time was composed of seven members. Betty, in her 70's, most often wore a dour expression, giving the impression that she carried the weight of the world on her shoulders and had to always swim upstream in life. Martha G, a pleasant Hispanic woman, was the board secretary. She said little but always sided with the DM. The board treasurer, Wayne W, was affable and well-spoken, a practicing CPA in town. He looked the part: neat black hair, bespectacled, and a clean cut appearance. I was told that he was a "company man" in that he usually sided with the prevailing views of the administration.

Then there was Wally, our new chairman, who remained an enigma to me. Outside of the board meetings he was cordial and talkative and had a pleasing chuckle. At board meetings, however, he appeared to take perverse pleasure in trying to put me down, a tactic that he often used on audience members as well. I presumed that this was his attempt to salve his own ego while trying to diminish, in particular, my influence. He obviously enjoyed wielding his power as chairman of the board. Jim warned me that I should not try to buck him in this endeavor as he appeared to be a master of this technique. I would lose if I tried to counter him. This didn't bother me. I didn't have a big ego that I had to protect and, by this age, I felt that my character and abilities would speak for themselves. I thought, too, that the audience would see this for what it was, an ego enhancing effort, and not a characteristic that would endear him to the crowd. I rather enjoyed trying to figure Wally out. This just added to my interest in deciphering how his clock ticked.

At the time, I thought that these were the four board directors who seemed aligned with Eve and who constituted a majority.

Board member Sue W, an attractive brunette, appeared to be an independent thinker with good judgment. I admired her thinking and felt that we likely would be supportive of one another. Insurance man Ken M, with his thick shock of gray hair, also on the board, held many of the district's insurance policies. From his remarks, I felt he was aligned with my thinking as well; however, I knew that he had to be careful not to alienate the DM for fear of losing the district's insurance business. He had been a director for three terms, almost twelve years, by far the longest of any of the board members. So, it seemed from a quick glance that there was a majority of four versus a minority of three to engage in whatever disputes might lie ahead.

COUNTERPOINT

Eve and Wally meet before the next board meeting where J.R. will be presenting his plan for a new clinic (speculation on my part of a conversation that might have occurred between Eve and Wally):

"Wally, what do you think about JR's presentation for a new clinic at the next board meeting?"

"I have to give him credit. He's jumping in with a plan for a private clinic before we have made any arrangements ourselves. We have to come up with our own clinic plan and pretty darn quick. He is trying to catch us off guard, thinking we'll buckle to him out of desperation. Do you have any ideas?"

"Well, Wally, I checked online and found a national company that sets up clinics and hospitals. I talked to one of their head guys, Bob

Bohlman, who said he could help us. I told him we could only pay $5000 max. He said that he could do it for that plus expenses. For our situation it would be a rather boilerplate plan, one that they use for rural areas."

"What about the time, Eve? Can he do it within the next month?"

"He can get on it right away. He has a vacation condo here in Pagosa, so he has a personal interest in getting this done the right way and getting it done now."

"Let's do it, Eve."

After the clinic resignations, the district appeared to be foundering; no plan had come forth for the future from either the administration or the board. Dr. Jim Knoll had some 25 years' experience in administrative medicine and in the past had dealt with many of the problems our district was presently undergoing. He came up with a "Six Point Plan" to give the district some direction. This was presented to the board and administration at a special board meeting in early May. Succinctly, the plan would: 1) allow the resigned physicians, Drs. Mark and Bob, to restructure their practice into a private clinic (this coincided with J.R. Ford's plan for a new, private clinic); 2) change the Dr. Mary Fisher Medical Center facility into a specialty care, same day surgery center plus lab facility; 3) reconfigure the Emergency Medical Service (EMS); 4) maintain the medical advisory committee (MAC) as a liaison between the district and the local physicians; 5) help in the recruitment of more local physicians; and 6) open a dialogue with Mercy Hospital in Durango to try to recoup some of the medical dollars leaving the county. These recommendations were to fill deficiencies now existing in the district's policies.

There was some discussion by the board and questions from the audience, but for the most part the consensus for accepting the plan was favorable. I made a motion that the plan be accepted as a district policy. It was adopted, unanimously. This was surprising in that no one questioned the setting up of a private clinic to replace the public clinic. Would this unanimity stick?[6]

At the regular board meeting later in May it was decided to give the clinic staff a 30-day extension from the date of their resignation, which would help both parties. This would give time for the administration to develop a plan, hire temporary physicians and staff, and give the resigned staff time to make arrangements of their own.

I knew the June board meeting would be eventful. J.R. Ford had been placed on the agenda and would be presenting his plan to take the clinic private. The town fire chief had indicated that the audience size was exceeding the fire code limits, so the board meetings were now moved to the new Community Center. The audience seemed to increase in size with each new meeting. I thought that was a good sign because it showed that the community was becoming more involved in what was going on in their health care district.

First on the agenda, the annual audit of our finances was presented for the year 2002 by an outside, independent auditor. "Remarkable ... superior" were his comments on the turnaround that had occurred during that year, in part due to the increase in the mil levy but also due to a decrease in expenses and an increase in revenue. Cash balance had gone from a deficit of $36,443 to $203,786 in the bank at the end of the year 2002. Kudos were showered by board members onto the clinic staff, EMS, and administration for a job well done. I thought it ironic to praise the clinic personnel when nothing had been done to preserve their future.[7]

J.R. Ford, fair-haired and in his forties, was then asked to present his plan for privatization of the Dr. Mary Fisher Clinic. I had heard that he was the manager of a large ranch in the area and that he ran several of his own businesses, including a land management company. What impressed me most about J.R. was that in the few meetings I had attended, he spoke clearly, to the point, and with good judgment. He gave an excellent Power Point presentation showing the financial arrangement for a new clinic and a forecast for business going two years forward. Their group would lease the clinic building, and the staff would consist of most of the former employees including the docs and the nurse practitioner. His financial statement showed how the clinic could be financially solvent right from the start. The board showed some enthusiasm for the plan. Their questions were mostly financial in nature. Eve and Wally remained silent.

Then Eve rose and said that she was proposing a plan, as well, and indicated that she had hired a consultant with broad experience in setting up clinics nationwide. The consultant was starting immediately on a plan that would consist of hiring *locum* physicians until permanent MD's could be found. A detailed plan would be forthcoming at the next board meeting. Seeing that a rather large amount of money and a contract were involved, I asked if the board should not have participated in making the decision to hire this consultant. Wally, in a demeaning fashion, said that the DM could spend up to $5000 without board approval and that this was the sum involved. This limit had been set by a previous board several years before. I got no answer about the board not being involved in this policy decision. Though new to corporate policy ways, I thought it only reasonable that a board should set the policy and be involved in contract negotiations, while the administration should implement that policy. I didn't pursue the matter further as I knew it would be a futile effort. It was apparent that the matter had already been decided by Eve and her supporters. It was again clear that the Eve had a stranglehold on the majority of the board members.

Jim and I talked to J.R. after the meeting, and we all agreed that his plan faced a strong headwind in view of Eve's forthcoming plan.

A few days later I received two contracts via email from our district's attorney for my review. One was a new employment contract for the DM and the other a contract for the operations manager of our Emergency Medical Service (EMS). I learned later that these contracts had been reviewed by the other board members before I took office. Interestingly, the title for the district manager was to be changed to executive director.* I was unaware of the reason for the change. The attorney had said to email him if we had any questions, so I queried the name change.

I received a call from Wally about this matter several days later. He was loudly irate that I had emailed our attorney.

"Don't you know he charges $400 an hour? You don't have the right to take his time and to incur this charge to the district."

At first I was speechless. Then I replied, "Wally, our attorney said to email him if we had any questions, which is what I did."

Wally went into a tirade about my not knowing what I was doing and that I should pay the district back for the charge incurred out of my own pocket. That sounded downright silly to me. He continued to rant and even said that he could have me thrown off the board. I was flabbergasted. I couldn't get a word in edgewise so I hung up. He called back immediately, still in a tirade, so I hung up again. The phone rang a third time. I didn't answer it. I could

---

* Eve's title was changed to executive director, but with the new board it reverted back to district manager. To avoid confusion, I have used district manager (or DM) throughout.

not believe this had happened. However, it showed me a side of Wally that would become more evident as time passed by.

When J.R. presented his plan to reopen the clinic as a private entity, he had requested four items from the administration, one of which was to rehire two of the employees who had recently been fired. Their replacements had no idea of how the billing and collections had been done previously, so this area was foundering. The old personnel, particularly these two, should be able to bring this situation under control in short order.

I had recently talked to the former employee who had been the billing clerk at the clinic. She indicated that she would go back if asked, since she could really use the money. Inasmuch as nothing had happened on J.R.'s request, I thought I would call Wally about the matter. I did not feel comfortable calling the DM, with whom I had had little contact so far. I voiced my concern about the billing and collections at the clinic to Wally and reminded him of J.R.'s request to rehire the two clerks. I suggested that we at least rehire the billing clerk.

"Dick, this is none of your business," he told me. "Keep your nose out of it. Let Eve do her job." He then went into another tirade, again saying that I didn't know what I was doing. I had been on the board just three months. I wondered what I had done to trigger this negative response. If there was anyone on the board to whom other members should be able to talk, it should be the chairman. Wally continued to rant, talking loudly over my attempts to reply. I hung up. Unbelievable—that this should happen again!

A week or so later, Ken Morrison, my fellow board member, called to say that Wally was calling the other board members and belittling me for calling him about these two matters. Why Wally was taking this belligerent attitude toward me was beyond my comprehension, particularly over two issues that anyone else would have discussed civilly.

After the June board meeting, a man with thinning gray hair and a rather scraggly beard came up to me and introduced himself. This was Norm Vance, the man in the red snowmobile whom Patti and I had met several months previously when we were out cross country skiing. At that time he had been bundled up, so now I didn't recognize him. With an anxious and quick manner, Norm indicated that he had formed a group in support of the district employees. They had been fighting to get fairer treatment. Norm's wife, Ruth, a nurse who had worked at the clinic, was now unemployed due to the mass resignations. He indicated that many of the critical comments that had come from the audience at the board meetings were from members of his group. This included the name I had heard as, "… way to go Toby," when I attended my first meeting and who subsequently had been very vocal in denouncing the administration. It also included Kay Grams, the board member and fire chief's wife, who had resigned from the board a few months previously. Norm indicated that his group was submitting recall petitions for all board members except for Wally and me. We were exempt from this process by virtue of the fact that we both had been appointed directors and not elected. Norm's group had also picked candidates whom they would nominate to replace the recalled directors. The petitions were about ready for submission to the county clerk. Feeling that I would be sympathetic with their thinking, Norm was seeking my support. I empathized with him. I remained noncommittal because I was still trying to find my way around this complex political maelstrom. I didn't want to further compromise my already delicate position on the board by openly aligning myself with Norm's group.

Just a week later our town newspaper, The *Pagosa Springs Sun*, revealed that the recall effort had failed. There were sufficient signatures on the petitions, some 200 names for each director to be recalled, but the failure was due to a technicality. Errors in the "circulator affidavits" had been made. Two inconsistencies were noted, one involving a date and the other an address.[8] On the one hand, these seemed to be trivial errors but the law had to be upheld. On the other hand, I would have thought that the originators of these petitions would have been meticulous in their preparations. Unfortunately, a lot of effort had gone for naught. I am sure that the board members named on the recall petitions breathed a sigh of relief.

In June, Jim and I made an appointment with Wally to discuss the district's problems. It had become obvious that Wally knew the background of the district quite well. We had also learned that he was a good friend of Eve and in fact, as a realtor, he had found a home for her when she had moved here from Lubbock, Texas, back in early 2002. Inasmuch as Wally was new to the board, too, it made sense to touch base with him and try to be conciliatory rather than be at logger heads with him, which is what was happening so far.

We met in Wally's real estate office, on the second floor of a building above a dentist's office. Rather drab and musty, it appeared not to be used very often. We spent most of the time explaining that we felt that the employees were being treated shabbily, particularly the clinic staff. We wondered if something could not be done, even at this late date, to resuscitate the clinic. We also brought up J.R.'s plan for a private clinic and how we were in favor of it in the absence of bringing the old clinic back to life. Wally listened patiently but was noncommittal about everything we mentioned. Afterwards, both Jim and I felt frustrated. Quite frankly, we didn't feel we had accomplished anything. However, we did set up a subsequent meeting with Wally in two weeks. That meeting was even more frustrating and yielded the same negligible result. Jim and I decided that it was fruitless to make any further effort in this direction. Also, the effort to be more conciliatory and friendly with Wally had no effect whatever on my and Wally's future board relationship.

I was informed that the board would hold two special board meetings or workshops in July. The first was for J.R. and his group to present their business plan for a private clinic again. Our DM, Eve, would have her consultant, Bob Bohlman, present to critique this plan. At the second session Bob Bohlman would present his and the administration's plan, and J.R. and his group could critique their plan. The board would be involved in reviewing both plans and would then vote to accept one of them. It sounded like a good agenda to me, and on the surface it seemed fair.

At the first meeting, J.R. and Dr. Mark presented their plan for a private clinic. The presentation was clear and concise, similar to what had been presented at the previous board meeting. It contained details on how the operation would work, the personnel, the funding to get started, and how the private clinic would interact with the district.

As J.R. spoke, I wondered how the new clinic could work with the administration after what had gone on previously, since personnel were still the same on both sides. Of course, the clinic would now be private so they could run things as they liked. But then, the clinic would be using tax levy money doled out by the district. That would be like having one's head in a guillotine, the blade ready to fall at Eve's whim. If the clinic could become independent and not need the tax money, then this burden would be lifted but when and if this could occur was a moot point now. Obviously, there were major challenges for the plan from both sides.

J.R.'s plan had an added feature. He had talked to the physicians in Dr. Jim Pruitt's Family Medicine Clinic and had arranged for the physicians in the two clinics to join together to provide 24/7 coverage, including nights and weekends. This was something the community had never had, but something it had been seeking for some time. It was a big plus and something we presumed that Eve's plan could not include, as there would be too few physicians to provide this coverage. There was virtually no chance that the local physicians would work with the temporary physicians brought in by Eve to provide this coverage. I should mention that the Family Medicine clinic docs did provide night and weekend coverage for their patients except for Friday and Saturday nights.

The discussion on the private clinic was entirely on financial grounds. Could it actually be fiscally feasible? The business plan did seem reasonable. All of the practicing physicians in the community would be involved in one way or another, so it behooved them to make it work. That was the strongest feature of the plan. Neither Wally nor Eve raised a question. I presumed that they were biding their time. Bob Bohlman, the developer of the district's plan, expressed his doubts about the financial feasibility of the private plan.

Jim and I talked to J.R. and his team after the meeting. We both thought it was an excellent plan. However, our underlying fear was that Eve's group had already made up their collective mind to the contrary. Inasmuch as they constituted the majority of the board, we did not have much hope they would accept J.R.'s plan over their own.

The second board meeting was one week later. Bob Bohlman, tall and bespectacled with thinning gray hair, had the demeanor of a confident professional. He had a good reputation, and he represented a national firm that planned both urban and rural clinics and hospitals. His presentation was straightforward and conservative, and for the most part it made sense. The clinic would open with one *locum* physician and a nurse practitioner. Additional medical personnel would be added as business increased. The process for recruiting a new, permanent physician would be started immediately to replace the *locum* MD. There was to be no after-hours coverage initially. It was a bare bones plan.

An important question was how the community would respond to either plan. On the one hand, you had a private clinic using local physicians. This should be at least as successful as the previous clinic in that the only difference was it was private rather than public. Quite frankly, the public would not see any difference. On the other hand, with the start of a new public clinic using *locum* physicians, there would be a big question of how successful the project could be. How accepting of the new, temporary physicians would the citizenry be? Why would a patient break off his or her already existing, longstanding patient-physician relationship for one that could only be of a temporary nature? Not likely! Also, any prospective new physician recruited by the district would surely talk to the local physicians and to community residents and discover the animosity that existed between the two groups. Why would any good physician want to come into this hostile environment? I had been a practicing physician, so this all seemed clear to me. However, I doubted that the DM reasoned this way. I did not doubt that she felt that she could pull this off and get a new clinic open and successful in a relatively short period of time—which would be essential to avoid a money drain on the district's finances.

The discussion following the presentation was benign. Bob Bohlman again critiqued J.R.'s plan and felt it was too expensive and that his plan was more likely to succeed. Wayne, our treasurer, supported Bob's comments. The major difference between the two plans was that J.R.'s plan had the added expense of including physician night and weekend coverage, which Bohlman's plan did not include. With or without the night and weekend coverage, J.R.'s plan appeared the more likely to be successful to Jim and me because the citizenry, quite obviously, would continue going to their prior physicians. This was our main criticism of the new public clinic. How were they going to attract new patients?

After the presentation and discussion had concluded, Betty immediately made a motion for the board to accept Bob Bohlman's plan. The vote was 4 to 3, the expected majority winning. It appeared that J.R. and his group's effort had been an exercise in futility. However, Jim and I applauded their effort.

Looking back on this event from three years forward, the private clinic would have avoided many of the problems that would subsequently occur and would have been a boon to the community—but here we are getting ahead of our tale.

One had to give Eve credit for coming up with a plan on short notice and using a credible source to develop it. This is what doomed J.R.'s plan. I had hoped that the district would have been desperate enough to accept the privatization plan in the absence of any other reasonable choice, but that had not happened. I had also thought that we might have come to some compromise on the privatization plan, such as dropping the 24/7 coverage to cut expenses initially—but the DM was going to have her new public clinic no matter what. She had the votes and that's all that counted.

Jim and I commiserated with J.R. and his team after the session. Dr. Mark indicated that he had been in talks with Dr. Jim Pruitt about joining their practice. Obviously he had been working on a backup plan for himself if the private clinic plan failed. This seemed like a good choice on his part. Of course he would take his patients with him, a further loss for the public clinic.

Jim and I agreed to meet at the DQ in a few days to discuss this outcome and to make plans for the future.

As an aside, I had sat next to Wally at the last workshop meeting. We had free time beforehand so we began discussing health care. I wondered whether he had any background in this area. He said that he had more experience in health care than I did. That floored me. I had retired from practicing medicine for 44 years just a few years previously. He wasn't old enough to have had this much experience even if all his adult life had been spent in health care. In fact, I could not tell that he had any experience in this area at all. At our board meetings he always deferred to the DM on health-related matters, and I couldn't recall one instance where he had offered any health care information or opinion. After this comment, I resolved to check into Wally's background for health care experience.

For that matter, I could not see that Eve had much health care experience either. Her words and actions had not demonstrated good judgment. I thought I should check into her background as well. Was I going too far as a board member? I wondered.

CHAPTER 5

STALEMATE

At the board meeting in July, Eve announced that she had hired a *locum* physician for the clinic. Shortly thereafter she hired a second *locum* physician and a nurse practitioner as well. In addition she was hiring separate *locum* physicians to cover weekends. This surprised me, as Bob Bohlman's plan was quite conservative, recommending hiring just one physician and a nurse practitioner initially until the practice could support more staff, and without after-hours coverage. I thought this was being extravagant. Although I had supported J.R.'s clinic plan, I had resolved, after Bob's plan was accepted by the board, that I would support it whole-heartedly. As a board member, that was my obligation, so I didn't raise any questions about this change at this time.

Sue W, one of the two board members who often shared my thinking at our meetings, announced that she was resigning as a director on the board. She had just been appointed to the position of civil engineer for the county, and this would take all her time. She didn't feel that she would be able to devote enough time to the district's business to be an effective director. I understood and wished her well, knowing that this left an even smaller like-thinking minority on the board.

Immediately, Wally announced that they already had a replacement for Sue's position. I spoke up reminding everyone that our by-laws outlined the procedure to be followed in choosing a new director. First we should advertise the position in the newspaper, then allow 30 days for applicants to apply. Finally we should interview the applicants before choosing a new director. That was the process used previously when Wally and I had been elected to the board. However, Wally said this was not necessary. I was appalled and at a loss for words. Obviously, Wally and Eve were going to ignore our by-laws to further their own ends.

Betty then nominated Laura Mitchell to be the new director. You will recall that Laura had been named head of the Citizen's Advisory Committee back in April. She had done a good job in that position, and I had nothing against her. However, I felt strongly that we should follow proper procedure in choosing the new director. Quickly, Wally asked if there were any further nominations. I thought of nominating Jim Knoll, but I knew that it would be a futile effort as Wally already had the votes to support Laura's nomination. I remained silent. The motion was made and voted upon, and Laura was elected by a four-to-two margin, Ken and I being the nays.

I remember Laura having said earlier at our first Citizen's Advisory Committee meeting that she was planning on running for county commissioner some time in the future. I wondered if she felt this was a stepping stone to that position. Laura, a perky, attractive and talkative woman, appeared younger than her middle-age years, and I thought her intelligent and well-spoken. She had tried to make the Citizen's Advisory Committee an active body. She had instigated, and the committee had worked on, bringing the local physicians to the point of providing 24/7 (night and weekend) coverage. The physicians had cooperated in the talks, but in the end they had declined to provide this coverage. I presumed that the local docs didn't trust the administration sufficiently to work with them. After the recent clinic imbroglio, one could hardly blame them. However, it was a good try, and its failure wasn't due to any lack of effort on the part of Laura or the committee.

Because Laura had done a good job as a committee chairwoman, I thought she deserved to be a director as well as anyone. But railroading her in came across as a pure power play, a need to demonstrate control. Eve, Wally, and their followers didn't seem to care what the community thought— or, for that matter, what their fellow board members thought. Pretty sad! This was a good example of why the community was so upset with the administration and the board and why they were so vocally critical at the board meetings.

Next on the agenda: Eve told us that she was hiring a consultant to evaluate our Emergency Medical Service (EMS). She said that there was considerable turmoil along with rumors that the entire service might resign, similar to what had happened at the clinic. That would be catastrophic as the EMS was the community's first line of defense in providing ambulance service for any accidents occurring in the Pagosa Springs District. Our EMS was also vital for picking up emergency patients for transport to the clinic or to Mercy Hospital in Durango, some 60 miles away.

It was obvious to me that there was considerable animosity between Eve and the emergency medical technicians (EMT's). This had been evident at the board meetings, with the EMT's voicing their concerns in public just as the clinic employees had done. Many of the EMT's had been fired, and more had resigned citing harassment by the district manager as the cause. A former board member, Kay Grams, had given me a list of EMT's who had been fired or quit since Eve had taken charge. The list was quite long. I knew some of these people, had talked to them, and had learned that many of them had been treated unfairly. This increased my resolve to continue fighting for what I felt was right. At the same time, I knew there was only so much this minority board member could do.

At this point, some three months into my tenure on the board, I thought I might try to forestall any mass exodus from the EMS. I had established a good relationship with some of the EMT's, particularly with the EMS manager, Kathy Conway. Rather than wait until a catastrophic event occurred, like the clinic exodus, I thought I might check with Kathy about their situation, though I felt ambivalent about taking this step. A member of the community had come up to me after one of the board meetings and had said that, as a board member, I should always support the majority decisions of the board. I had been very vocal in supporting J.R.'s plan and opposing Eve's plan, but after Eve's plan had passed, I never said I would not support it even though I felt in the end it would fail. I had voiced strong opposition to several other prospective board policies, but once motions were passed, I had supported them. I knew that the chain of command was for the board to direct the administration and then let the administration deal directly with the employees. A board director should not bypass management, as I was thinking of doing. On the other hand, I was only conversing with an employee, not giving direction. In view of the bad relationship between the board and the employees, I thought it would be good for the employees to know that they had at least one supporter on the board. Furthermore, the administration had already broken this chain of command by undermining the board's authority. I couldn't be a passive director, particularly when I saw the district headed on a downhill course. I felt I had to be an activist and try to change the direction of a ship heading into a storm.

Kathy, a dark-haired, athletically attractive and energetic woman, had been elevated to the EMS operations manager position several months previously from the ranks of the EMT's. Even in this short time, she and Eve had disagreed on several occasions. They were not on good terms now. Besides the employee problem, it appeared that Eve wanted to micro-manage everything under her wing, whether she had the expertise in the area or not. Dr. Pruitt, who saw many of the emergency patients, had counted 31 instances where Eve had interfered with medical decisions.

An egregious event occurred this same month, when Dr. Bob met a patient at the emergency room in the Dr. Mary Fisher Medical Center at night for treatment. As the physician director of the EMS, Dr. Bob had permission to use these facilities. For some reason, Eve called the police saying someone had broken into the clinic. The police investigated and interrogated Dr. Bob in front of his patient, which was very embarrassing for him, making it look like he did not have permission to use the facility. He had been harassed by Eve before this situation, having been one of the physicians who had recently resigned from the clinic. This brought Dr. Bob to the breaking point, and he resigned as physician advisor to the EMS. Eve couldn't find a physician in the immediate area to fill Dr. Bob's vacated position. She had to go to Cortez, 100 miles to the west of town, to find a new physician advisor for the EMS. This was a poor and risky choice because of the distance involved, particularly in an emergency situation. This blew my mind, since there was no rational explanation for this behavior on the part of the DM.

On contacting Kathy, she voiced many of the concerns that I had heard from the clinic personnel. Employees were spoken to harshly, several had been fired unjustly, and many had quit because they couldn't take the harassment any longer. Although there had been talk of a mass resignation among the EMT's, they agreed that patient care came first. They felt responsible. For them, should they quit, the district's only backup would be the emergency services from neighboring communities. The increased burden to those services and the distances involved would put any emergency situation in our area at increased risk. So, while they considered a mass resignation, there was no real threat of this actually occurring. Also, at this time Kathy felt somewhat protected from Eve's fury by the fact that Eve knew that the EMT's might well all resign if she were fired. It appeared that Kathy had the situation under control, at least for the present.

Later in the month we learned that Eve had chosen Allan Hughes to be the EMS consultant. He had been an EMT himself and now ran a consulting service out of Denver concerning EMS affairs. He came and spent several days at the end of July, interviewing the EMS personnel, talking to the administration, and going over records regarding finances, information on ambulance runs, and other issues.

One further meaningful event occurred at the July board meeting. Just two months previously, Dr. Jim Knoll had presented his "Six Point Plan" to the board and this had been accepted without dissent. As mentioned previously, we were surprised by its acceptance as the report had recommended setting up a private clinic which, of course, had not happened. Jim reminded the board of their prior commitment to his plan. Betty immediately made a motion to rescind this prior document. This passed by majority vote. To show his thorough disgust with this decision, Jim resigned his position as head of the MAC. Without his leadership, the local physicians in town were no longer interested in participating, and the MAC died. What little influence the local docs might have had on the board died with this action and the schism between the local docs and the district widened. Jim and I continued to meet with the local docs thereafter from time to time to keep each other abreast of what was of mutual concern to all of us.

Our local newspaper, The *Pagosa Springs Sun*, followed the events of the health district very closely and about this time its respected editor, Karl Isberg, wrote an editorial wherein he stated that he was expressing the sentiment of many Pagosans. "The cast of the ongoing soap opera we know as the 'Upper San Juan Health Service District Show' continues to deliver award-winning performances, but it is a show in desperate need of cancellation."[9] He was appalled by the timidity of the board to take decisive action and said, were it not for serious ramifications, their performance would be comic. He questioned the recent controversial decision to open a new public clinic, and he indicated that this decision would be judged at the next election of board directors. This proved to be a prescient call.

CHAPTER 6

THE GENERAL AND THE FOOT SOLDIER

In late July, Jim and I met again for lunch at the DQ. Health care in Pagosa was on Jim's mind much of the time, as it was on mine. He felt that medicine and health care in Pagosa were still in a 1960's mode. We had good physicians, a modern clinic facility, and an excellent private clinic next door to it, all good basics from which to develop.

However, we remained an isolated rural community that didn't take advantage of state or federal programs that had been set up to help rural areas throughout the country. There was no integration of the different health care entities, either in the community or with programs in the surrounding area. Nor did we have a beneficial relationship with our closest neighboring medical facility, Mercy Hospital in Durango.

From the "Six Point Plan" that Jim had developed in the spring, he now fleshed out a vision for the future of health care in Pagosa and, importantly, how we might get there. This looked beyond the present board, which we now saw as a stumbling block for any future progress. The plan consisted of three parts, the first of which was a Position Statement; "… to move us out of a fragmented system into a Comprehensive Integrated Healthcare System": 1) to support our medical providers we need to improve the relationship between the local docs and the district; both with the Board and with management. The district should be involved with the local physician groups in recruiting medical personnel for the community as the need arises. 2) The Dr. Mary Fisher Medical Center (clinic) should be expanded to include better diagnostic services and to include specialty clinics. Both the public and private clinics should be encouraged to share equipment and services to avoid unnecessary duplication and expense. 3) The Emergency Medical Service should be revamped. Mercy Hospital in Durango, 60 miles away, has a large, highly qualified emergency medical group. We should contract with their ER group to provide medical oversight, up-to-date training of our EMT's, and we should use standardized emergency protocols consistent with their procedures inasmuch as the majority of our emergency ambulance patients are taken to their facility. 4) Standing committees, such as finance, should be established, comprised of local citizens to advise the board and management and to act as a check and balance among the board, management and the public. The Medical Advisory Committee (MAC) should be re-established to act as a liaison between the district and the local physicians. 5) Last, but certainly not least, the district should develop a close and strong working relationship with Mercy Hospital in Durango. There are benefits for both parties; Mercy Hospital gets a large influx of patients from our area to fill their beds. They, in turn, to ensure this flow, should be willing to provide us with expert advice and help in providing specialists for our clinics.

The second part of Jim's plan involved the board of directors. Jim emphasized to me that it would be essential to have an accommodative board of directors to implement "The Position Statement." The next election was in May 2004, still some ten months away, but it was not too early to start looking for board of director candidates to run in that election. Six of the seven board positions would be expiring. Jim proposed finding a slate of six candidates who would all support the Position Statement. These six nominees would run on the same platform as one body. The electorate would see these candidates as all having the same purpose and, hopefully, vote for them as a group. This would then give the board the strength to put into effect the five elements of the Position Statement.

The third part of Jim's vision was to begin setting up our own committees now that could be formalized as board committees if and when we were elected. These committees-in-waiting could start functioning now by formulating the policies that would be implemented when we took office. The committees were: Finance, Rules and By-laws, Medical Advisory, Citizen's Advisory, and EMS (Emergency Medical Services). I thought it might be a little presumptuous to set up these committees now but, as time would show, it was very anticipatory.

Until his retirement, Jim had been head of the Department of Psychiatry at Presbyterian Hospital, as well as a professor in the Department of Psychiatry at Southwestern Medical Center, both in Dallas, Texas. As part of the Presbyterian Healthcare System, he had been intimately involved in setting up clinics across north Texas, giving him an insight into the type of problems that we were now encountering in Pagosa Springs.

I was impressed by this plan. I thought we were fortunate

Jim and Ingrid Knoll with Patti and Dick Blide

to have someone of Jim's caliber and experience to give us this vision. He was to become our guru, our general, in the battles that were to come. I was energized by Jim's plan, which gave us a clear, concrete direction that we could start acting on right now.

Over the summer we began implementing all of these proposals. We made a dozen or so revisions to the Position Statement until we felt it was a lean, clear, and strong statement. In the ensuing six months, we interviewed many board candidates over lunch. For the most part, Jim chose the candidates. Assuming the role of an executive secretary, I set up the appointments and made the arrangements. Some of the interviewees were not interested, usually because they were too busy or they didn't want to become embroiled in what was now viewed as an unsavory political situation. But we did find some outstanding candidates who felt strongly that changes were needed in the health district.

Jim began establishing the committees, which was an easier task as these members would have much less political involvement. It became very clear that there were many in the community who were cognizant of the problems in the health district and aware of the dire need to improve the situation. I was impressed by many of these individuals who, though very busy, felt that it was their duty to give some of their valuable time to improving health care in their community.

I realized that I was becoming more and more contentious at board meetings, making me feel somewhat uncomfortable. I had no choice but to speak up when other board members said something with which I disagreed. On one occasion a member of the audience came up to me after a meeting and said that he thought I should be more supportive of board actions. I asked Jim whether he felt that I was acting appropriately as a board member. My thinking was that I should be supportive of board decisions once they became policy. However, if I felt that a board action was clearly wrong, fiscally or medically, I should voice my concern. Jim felt this was the correct posture and supported what I had done previously. He realized I was in a difficult position, with little support on the board and none from the administration. Thoughts of resigning as a director crossed my mind more than once. However, I also realized that I was now beginning to represent the medical community on the board. Medical personnel had never had a voice on the board at any time in the past. In fact, one former board member mentioned to me that those in control of the board in the past had not wanted a doctor on the board: "We were afraid that a doc would try to take over. Anyway, it's 80 percent business and only 20 percent medicine." Such were the thoughts from the past. So, even if I were but a token doc on the board, it was a first step forward. To me this seemed the right thing to do. Now, and especially later, the support that Jim and others in the community gave me were paramount in keeping me going. They let me know that I was not alone in what was shaping up to be an epic battle between two diametrically opposing ideologies.

In the ensuing month, I began to wonder if I was becoming too agreeable to Jim's plan and vision for the future. Should I be making more of a contribution, doing some creative thinking myself? I realized that I had become completely absorbed in the everyday happenings of the district, which I considered a pretty normal reaction under the circumstances. I wondered if I were somewhat envious of Jim's accomplishments.

At our next lunch at the DQ Jim asked if something was wrong. He obviously had sensed a subtle change in my attitude. He was very astute and sensitive, skills he had undoubtedly honed in his practice as a psychiatrist. We had become good friends very rapidly, not only because of our intense and common interest in the deteriorating health care situation, but also because we had a common bond from both being physicians. Beyond that, we seemed to think alike and to have common likes and dislikes. I now felt unsettled for having these ambivalent thoughts; perhaps a little jealousy on the one hand while being supportive on the other. I denied to Jim at that time that anything was wrong, and he let it go.

After this meeting, I sat at my desk at home to sort out my thoughts. Without question, Jim had come up with a brilliant vision and plan for the district's future. That was obvious to me. I knew that for Jim's plan to be successful it would require a joint effort of many dedicated people and a lot of hard work. I wanted to be a part of that team. Showing his leadership skills, Jim would be our general and I would be a foot soldier in the army, battling to accomplish his vision. This would become my passion for the foreseeable future. I don't believe that Jim ever doubted my intentions again.

As I mentioned previously, Norm Vance headed a group that included many of the employees and their families of the EMS and the Mary Fisher Clinic, seeking better and fairer treatment for the employees. They were the ones most vocal at the board meetings in disagreeing with the DM and the board. About this time, one of the board members in the majority accused me of bringing my "gang" with me to board meetings, as the audience was always supportive of my thinking and verbally critical of Eve, Wally, and their cohorts. Of course, Norm and his group had been here long before I appeared on the scene, and I had nothing to do with their coming to our board meetings. In rebuttal I asked where were their supporters and why didn't they attend the meetings? I received no answer. Significantly, the crowds at the board meetings continually grew larger, obviously becoming quite diverse and not representing any one group. By the summer and fall months, the audience size must have at least trebled compared to when I first began attending these meetings at the beginning of the year.

We asked Norm to head the Citizens Advisory Committee-in-waiting, and he brought with him several of his workers who had helped in the recall attempt. Their goal would be to try to involve the citizenry in the future planning for healthcare in the district. The other committees were fleshed out as well. J.R. was placed on the Finance Committee, which was headed by Dave B, an astute financial mind. This committee would become integral to our future success.

CHAPTER 7

A LITTLE DETECTIVE WORK

I had been told by the former board chairman, Dick Babillis, that the board had chosen Eve to be district manager of the health service back in '02 because she had an MBA and had healthcare experience as well, having been the director of the Student Health Service at Texas Tech University. She had come with good references, principally from some of the physicians who had worked at the health service's clinic.

In her first year on the job in Pagosa she had shown good financial skills by bringing the district out of the financial morass she had inherited. She was helped in no small measure by the former chairman, who was instrumental in getting the electorate to increase the mil levy, thereby significantly raising the tax base for the district. Eve also hired a CPA to be the financial officer for the district, which proved to be a wise move.

On the other hand, she had demonstrated poor people skills in handling the employees. In addition, she had alienated all of the local practicing physicians, who were the heart of the local healthcare system. Yet, in meeting with her personally and in small groups, I saw that she could be personable and charming. I was in a quandary about our DM and felt the need to obtain a better understanding of her thinking and motivation. I decided to check into her background.

I called Texas Tech University and was able to reach someone high in the administration of the Student Health Service. This person had known Eve well. At first she was reluctant to give out any information, but then she said that I could obtain Eve's personnel record from their office under the Texas Open Records Act. This act permitted anyone to obtain records from a state public institution upon request. I requisitioned a copy of this record through the university's attorney.

Eve had been with the university 10 years. She had then been promoted to Administrative Director of the Student Health Service two years prior to taking the position with us. The service had a separate medical director so her duties were solely of an administrative nature. Perusing the records further revealed that Eve had received kudos for good performance which resulted in her promotion. However, in the two years as administrative director she had received two reprimands. These were for taking a matter over the head of her superiors to university executives outside her department. She had requested a change in the department structure without first seeking the approval of her immediate superiors or even making them aware of her intentions. This tendency to skirt the rules and to make decisions based solely on her own thinking or feelings rather than first consulting with her contemporaries and superiors seemed egocentric to me. It was consistent with her behavior with us and not a good harbinger for our future.

By this time, I was accumulating a considerable amount of information on the health district as I thought it important to know its history, not only the actions that had taken place but also about the people involved. I continued to dig further for more information.

Ken Morrison and I had been of like thinking at board meetings. As an alert and focused person, he manifested a serious nature, at the same time coming across as being open and sociable. I presumed that his demeanor had been formed in his insurance business, where he appeared to be quite successful. Knowing that Ken had been on the board for almost 12 years, I called and asked if he had kept district records over this period of time. He said that he had kept every scrap of paper he had ever been given. That really whetted my appetite. When I asked if I could look through his archives, he said I was more than welcome to look at everything he had on file.

When I visited Ken in his office the next day, he brought out a huge stack of notebooks and papers. I saw that he had not exaggerated. It appeared that he had squirreled away every piece of paper associated with the district. Ken gave me a desk to use. I had done research in my earlier academic medical days and had discovered that I relished ferreting out details. So, this was like receiving a gift, a treasure trove into which I could delve.

The most revealing item I discovered was the résumé submitted by Wally when he had applied for a board seat just several months previously. In it he claimed, "I have 25+ yrs experience in Hospital and Clinic Administration…." That really piqued my interest. You will recall that Wally had claimed earlier in the month, just before one of the board meetings, that he had more health care experience than I.

It was with great anticipation that I decided to check into Wally's background also. I knew he had lived in Pagosa for 12 or 13 years but I knew of nothing previous other than that he was from the Houston area. So, I called an old friend in Dallas who had been a federal secret service agent and in retirement now ran a security business. He recommended that I hire a detective, and he gave me the name of one in Denver whom he knew and recommended highly. I called this detective and gave him the only information I had, that Wally was probably from the Houston area. Surprisingly, he called back within the week. His inquires had found that Wally was indeed from the Houston area, he was divorced, and his former wife still lived in that area. The detective had contacted her and fortunately she was forthcoming with information. She stated that Wally had attended college and afterwards had obtained a position with NCR Corporation, selling computer systems to medical institutions. He had held this position to about the time of their divorce. The wife was less clear about his employment thereafter, but she was aware that he had held several different positions with some being outside the State of Texas. She was not aware that he had ever worked in any type of healthcare organization.

On one occasion Wally had mentioned to Jim Knoll and me that he had taken an internship at Presbyterian Hospital in Dallas. I presumed that this was a business health care-related type of training. He even mentioned that he had had a chance to scrub in on several operations. This training actually was represented as occurring while Jim K was at the same institution. Jim had neither met nor heard of Wally Perkins during this time. Perhaps his "internship" was of short duration.

Checking locally, I discovered that, when Wally first came to Pagosa, he had opened a business that sold television satellite services. In fact, several people mentioned that they had used this service with satisfaction. This business had since gone by the wayside. He had also opened and currently ran an Italian restaurant in town with a relative actually managing the business. In addition, he had a real estate business. Wally appeared quite industrious.

To learn that our board chair had virtually no healthcare experience after claiming that he had more than I did was disturbing and sent up a red flag. Giving him the benefit of doubt, I suppose he was equating selling computer systems to hospitals and clinics with the experience one might obtain from working in a health care organization. Hardly! His apparent purpose had been to make it appear that he had some expertise in the health care area. After all, how many people actually check into a person's background to see if their claims are true? This would explain why he deferred to Eve on health-related issues. He had no such experience to fall back on.

Wally was obviously intelligent, well spoken, and charming. Why then did he need to present himself as someone he was not? Then there was the belligerence he showed toward the audience and me at our board meetings and the need to intimidate those with whom he disagreed. I supposed this was a matter of ego and a sign of insecurity . . . but it was perhaps more.

I had recently read David L. Weiner's book, *Power Freaks: Dealing With Them In The Workplace Or Anyplace.*[10] Therein the author describes the person who works in a subordinate position exhibiting normal work characteristics, then on being elevated to a position of authority, often changes behavior and becomes excessively controlling to the degree that it becomes harmful to the entire workplace and business. On a grander scale some of these individuals develop a reputation and are actually sought after by other companies to help them solve their problems . . . to the company's detriment. Look at the "Power Freaks" who came into control during the stock market bubble in the '90s, at Sunbeam, Enron and WorldCom, and the harm they wrought. I feared that we were seeing a duopoly exhibiting similar, excessive control but on a smaller, local scale.

I decided that these two background checks gave me a much better insight into the current problems of the district. There was a dearth of knowledge, experience and particularly good judgment at the top executive level. In administration this was exhibited through the employee problem, and in the medical area this was shown by the lack of insight in setting up the new clinic, specifically not understanding patient-physician relationships. The latter, at least, could have been prevented by their consulting with the medical expertise available in the community, namely the local docs in practice, the retired physicians, and the other healthcare professionals—to say nothing of this retired doc on the board. The need to control and exert power appeared to be the driving force behind the decision-making now taking place to the detriment of good governance.

I presented all this information to Jim at one of our DQ lunches. Not surprised at these findings, he felt that they were consistent with the behavior we were seeing in the board and administration now. He didn't think we could effect any change until the next election, which was still some ten months away. Being more impetuous, I wanted to try for change before then, though the means for doing so weren't evident, at least not at this time.

CHAPTER 8

A BOLT OUT OF THE BLUE

On a personal note, one day in early August Patti came to me saying she had something to show me. She had felt a vaginal discharge. She showed me a piece of Kleenex with blood on it. This brought a lump to my throat and a feeling of dread. We immediately made an appointment with her gynecologist. Her exam was negative but we had to wait for the pathology report of her Pap smear. It came back positive for uterine cancer. We had steeled ourselves but when the news actually arrived we were both devastated, our worst fear coming true. I was aware that we could hardly do better than the M.D. Anderson Cancer Center in Houston, Texas, for diagnostic services and treatment. I called, got the Gynecology Department, and made an appointment for Patti to see one of their cancer docs. We flew down to Houston and several days later saw Dr. Bodurka, a gynecologist who specialized in female cancers. Meanwhile, the Pap smear from home had been sent to another lab to verify the diagnosis, which was corroborated.

Patti's workup showed no evidence of spread of her cancer. Dr. Bodurka was involved in a research study tracking the lymphatic drainage from the uterus. She asked permission to include Patti in her study. This involved injecting dye and a radioisotope into the uterus before removing it surgically and then tracking its dissemination via the lymphatic system. We saw no reason to say no, so Patti was included in the study. I only mention this now because of subsequent events. Patti had a total hysterectomy and all went well. We felt that she had a cure but, of course, only time would tell.

We were fortunate that we were able to stay at the Rotary House, a hotel attached to the center. This facility, geared toward cancer patients and their families, gave exceptional service to everyone. This allowed Patti to get out of the hospital earlier and to recuperate more comfortably while waiting for our flight back to Pagosa Springs. This whole episode happened in a period of two weeks. We were very grateful to have things go so rapidly and smoothly and at one of the best cancer centers in the country.

CHAPTER 9

A CIRCUS WITHOUT COTTON CANDY

I missed the August board meeting because we were in Houston. The only matter of consequence to occur was J.R. asking whether the EMS consultant's report had arrived yet as the study had been completed several weeks previously. This was an important query because of events yet to come. Eve said that they had received a preliminary report but she didn't want to release anything until the final report was available.

The *Pagosa Springs Sun* described the September board meeting as "… a circus without the benefit of cotton candy or elephants."

It started even before the minutes from a series of previous meetings could be approved—the second item on the agenda after establishing a quorum. "Don't shake your head, Dan," Board Chairman Walter said to Dan K, who was sitting in the audience with the rest of the public. Dan, Family Medicine Clinic nurse practitioner, is a former employee of the district and now works for a private family medicine practice in the community. Dan and the rest of the audience had been sitting quietly up to that point. (In a later interview, Dan said he was shaking his head because of the number of corrections being made to a long list of minutes) After Walter's comment, Dan got up and left the room. The rest of the crowd began laughing.

During the laughter, Perkins made a comment to another member of the audience, Jim S. who replied with, "I can laugh if I want to." The two argued back and forth for a few moments, their voices escalating.

"Get the officer to escort this man out," Walter screamed at one point. A Pagosa Springs officer entered and asked Jim Sawicki to leave. Jim did.

Audience members vocally expressed their displeasure.

"Are we going to get back to business or are we going to listen to these people who don't matter?" Walter said. That led to an outright uproar.

"I won't tolerate this nonsense," Walter said. "If I have to clear the room I will."

"You can't" and "Go ahead and try," were some of the responses heard in the community center conference room.

Walter replied that he could have the whole audience of 40 – 50 removed, "because this is my meeting, not yours."

One woman screamed for the officer to come back in and escort Walter out, others yelled directly at the board. The officer returned, asking everyone to calm down.

Eventually the board returned to approving the minutes and then committee reports."[11]

After this uproar, board member Betty apologized for Wally, saying that he had been under considerable strain. Wally himself then apologized. My reaction to this one-act play was first disbelief, then amusement and finally sadness.

That was the center ring. The theatrics were not quite over yet, and another show was about to ensue in a side ring. Raucousness to a lesser degree occurred when new board member Laura, now strongly in step with Eve, brought up some comments that I had made at a League of Women's Voters (LWV) meeting the week before. This meeting had been scheduled to debate the health care issues between the two sparring parties: the local physicians and me versus those in control of the Board, Wally and Eve. At the last minute Wally and Eve had withdrawn, saying they had a conflict. The district had a workshop scheduled for 4 pm the same day, and the LWV meeting was at 7 pm. I doubted that there would actually be an overlap, and there wasn't. I was able to attend both sessions. I think the real reason for their canceling was that the district had no vision for the future, so they would have nothing to present for debate.

Dr. Jim Pruitt presented an excellent, detailed, and enlightening history of medical care in the community. Going back 20 years, when he first began practice, he had a great vision for the future, much of which had not yet come to pass.

At the beginning of my talk I clearly stated that I was speaking as a knowledgeable, private citizen and not as a board director. During my talk, and after a long explanation, I had referred to the majority of the board as being, "deaf, dumb, and blind." I was inferring, of course, that the majority of the board listened to no one, they didn't speak to the citizens about the latter's concerns, and they were blind to seeing where they were leading the district. I also called for the resignation of both the DM and the chairman of the board because of the disastrous downhill course on which they were leading the district.

Halfway through my LWV talk, I saw Laura walk into the auditorium. She never heard my initial disclaimer saying that I was speaking as a private citizen. Now, at the board meeting she was saying that I had made these remarks as a board member, which broke our rules and as such was unacceptable. Audience members who had heard my talk and disclaimer came to my support and corrected her misconception. This remark may not have been the most diplomatic thing for me to say but I was becoming more and more incensed by the words and actions of this "Gang of Four" and their total disregard for what seemed correct and proper and particularly for the concerns of the community. I had wanted to say something that would get noticed and awaken the people of the community to the travesty that was occurring before their eyes.

After this exchange, Laura asked if I was going to continue with my "negativity." I told her that at every level of government a voice of dissent is allowed to be heard. Many times it is the voice of accountability.

I later recalled Laura's words as I read Edward Mendelson's book, *The Things That Matter,* where he said, "Unity is a goal with no ethical meaning, an appealing sounding but impossible condition that in the real world of emotional and political life is sought mostly by sentimentalists and tyrants. Equality, in contrast, is a difficult but plausible goal, with profound emotional and ethical meaning in both the private and the public one."[12] I thought this apropos for our situation. Eve wanted me to join the unity she had with Wally, Betty, Laura, and Martha, similar to what she had before I had joined the board. I thought this incongruous as it was the opposite of what she had given her superiors when she was at Texas Tech. According to the written record, she had gone over the heads of her superiors to make a recommendation that they obviously would not have approved. Then, it seemed, she wanted equality and wasn't willing to give unity, the same equality that she was denigrating me for now through Laura. Did she see the contradiction in this behavior? Or was it supposed to be "do as I say not as I do?"

This was the rowdiest and most raucous meeting we would have, though others later would come pretty close. Interestingly, many of these meetings were tape recorded. The district kept minutes of all meetings and the weekly newspaper reported on all meetings and archived its articles. At election time, months down the road, Wally's comments from this meeting would still echo in many citizens' ears.

This meeting with all its antics triggered an editorial in the local paper, The *Pagosa Springs Sun*: "…your current leadership is too confrontational, too lacking in diplomatic skills … ." Karl Isberg, the editor, recalled one of the health district's stated core values, "Leadership at all levels: challenging the process, inspiring vision and leading the way." He stated, "It's time for a change to produce that leadership." He also appealed to the health district board and management to listen to expertise in the medical field from the local practicing docs, the retired docs, and the medical administrators living in the community.[13]

This editorial had no impact on the board or management, but it gave voice to what many in the community were thinking.

On a more positive note, three of the personnel who had been a part of the mass clinic resignation several months previously were now opening the Pagosa Women's Health and Wellness Clinic headed by nurse practitioner Susan Kuhns, with nurse Ruth Vance and businesswoman Terry Sellers. They had leased an old building across town and had revamped it themselves. Shortly thereafter Dr. Bob opened his practice in the same building with them. It was very heartening to see these individuals rise above that fiasco and flourish. Many of us visited them and wished them well.

CHAPTER 10

OUT-OF-TOWN PERSPECTIVE

In the early fall, Jim Knoll, Dick Babillis, and I paid a visit to Dr. Don Bader, the head of the emergency medical service at Mercy Hospital in Durango. This meeting was for the dual purposes of seeing if they could be of any help to our EMS presently and/or help us in the future when a new board might be in place.

Don, young and athletic in appearance, met us wearing scrubs and running shoes. His private group of about a dozen ER physicians had contracted with Mercy to run their emergency services. He was friendly and open in his feelings about our health district. Mercy Hospital received the majority of our emergency ambulance runs, so Dr. Bader was quite aware of the status of our EMS, particularly on the care given by our EMT's. He was not happy with their performance and felt that only two of our paramedics were presently performing at an acceptable level.

We asked if he and his group would participate in a teaching program for our EMT's and help us with other parts of our service. In view of our present board and management problems, particularly the political situation, he said that he was not inclined to get involved in any aspect of our service at this time. However, he would be more than willing to help us once the political situation improved. We were not surprised by this attitude. It did show that we could likely expect their help once we had resolved our own problems, hopefully by instituting a regime change in the spring.

Not long afterward, Jim and I also visited the CEO of Mercy Hospital, from whom we received exactly the same message. He showed us the plans for a new Mercy Hospital to be built on the edge of Durango and closer to Pagosa Springs, which would make the trip between the two towns a few miles shorter than the current 60 miles. We shared their enthusiasm, and I believe we both felt a little envious of their vision for their future.

Around this same time Dick Babillis and I visited the health service district in Telluride, Colorado, about 100 miles to our west. They were about the same size as Pagosa, as well as being a resort community, so we wondered if they might have problems similar to our own. They had a clinic and EMS, as did we, though their EMS was larger and busier than ours due to a larger tourist business in both the winter and summer months. The Telluride district had been a subdivision of the hospital in Montrose, Colorado, some 65 miles to their north. In the spring they had been notified that this association would cease due to a continuing loss in revenue from Telluride. This information came as a shock, and since then they had been scrambling to get reorganized.

We met with a new district manager, who had been hired just a month previously. One of their emergency docs had taken charge and was leading the board's effort to get back on solid footing. We met with him, too, and between the two of them we received a good idea of how they were solving their problems. It was enlightening to see how aggressively a small town our size could grasp their problem, come up with solutions, and then implement them. It gave us hope that we could do the same.

I was impressed by the fact that they had just purchased an expensive new CT scanner. This was something that we, too, desired, but it was way beyond our means presently. Thinking creatively, they had organized a summer music festival which had produced an excellent profit, providing the down payment for this equipment. This festival would become a stable, annual source of funds. Pagosa already had one summer music festival but could probably carry another one. Thinking this might be a good source of funds for us, too, I stashed the idea away in my memory bank for future reference.

Around this same time, Jim and I had lunch in Durango with the head of the Regional Emergency Medical & Trauma Advisory Council (RETAC) for southwest Colorado, Nancy Fulleur. This state regional organization coordinated EMS services. Having conversed with her by phone on several occasions, I had been impressed by her knowledge and vision.

Christina's Restaurant in Durango, one of Patti and my favorite places to go for a palate-savoring dining experience, was chosen as the site for this meeting. It was another beautiful, cool, sunny day, allowing us to sit outside under the trees, providing ambiance in a secure and comfortable setting.

It appeared that Nancy was in the cat bird's seat, getting both sides of the story of our district's affairs. Our district manager, Eve, was on Nancy's board of directors, as was one of our former paramedics, Crystal Coughlin. Crystal had recently quit working with our EMS due to continuing harassment from Eve and, as a single mom, she felt the need for more security. Crystal had found a similar job in a neighboring community. Seemingly as a reprisal, Eve was trying to have Crystal removed from the RETAC board, but Nancy said Crystal could not be let go until her term expired. Crystal could have resigned, but she had no intention of doing so, if for no other reason than to spite Eve. I understood and admired Crystal's bravado.

According to Nancy, interested parties throughout the state were following our district's dilemma. I knew that the EMT's were a close knit group and that they had a wide network of communications, so the existence of an active rumor mill was no surprise.

In these three instances, talking to Mercy, to the Telluride group, and to Nancy, I felt we had obtained a better perspective of where our district stood with respect to health care in small, rural, neighboring communities. Obviously, our district was not well thought of either in our own town, in the surrounding area or, in fact, throughout the state. We had work to do.

CHAPTER 11

A NEW CRISIS

In early October our EMS operations manager, Kathy Conway, called to ask if I would come in on Saturday to be present while she discharged one of the male EMT's. She made it clear that the man had to be dismissed immediately because he had treated an emergency patient inappropriately. Because Kathy didn't feel comfortable doing this alone and due to the fact that no one else was available, she called me. As a board member, I didn't feel comfortable overstepping the district manager, who was out of town, but the immediacy seemed to make this necessary. I did wonder though, "Why me?"

The dismissal of the EMT occurred uneventfully. He was a big, burly guy so I could see why Kathy wanted some support. More importantly, it's always wise to have a witness present in this type of situation.

Immediately afterwards, Kathy mentioned that John Farnsworth, the district's financial manager, was waiting down the hall and wanted to speak to me. I then realized that Kathy had had another motive in asking me to come in on this day.

John, a middle-aged, affable person, was a CPA who had practiced accounting in Minnesota as well as here in Pagosa. I had spoken to John on several occasions about the district's finances, and I had always found him to be pleasant and informative.

John got right to the point. He was disturbed by the deteriorating finances in the district. The expenses of the clinic had escalated greatly on hiring the *locum* physicians, not only because of their higher salaries, but also from ancillary expenses such as travel, room and board. At the same time, income from the clinic was on a downhill trajectory. Furthermore, Dr. Wienphal was moving his practice over to the private Family Medicine Clinic imminently and would be taking his patients with him, further eroding income. The clinic was becoming a "black hole," sucking up all available funds from the district's coffers.

No sooner had the financial books for August been closed by John than Eve had brought him a large stack of unpaid bills and requisitions, "six inches high," John told me, which would accelerate the money drain. John did not see anything that could improve this situation in the near term, and he saw a financial crisis looming in the next few months. His confidence in the district manager had fallen to the point where he felt the need to share this information with a board member, but not one of Eve's "people."

I asked John if he had brought this looming debacle to Eve's attention. He had, but she was determined to follow her present course no matter what the consequences might be. John then said that at the last board meeting someone had left their briefcase behind and it had been found while the district personnel were putting away the tables and chairs. This had been handed to Eve. She indicated to John that it contained papers indicating that a prominent group of town citizens were forming an alliance against her and her supporters, planning to take over at the next election (I subsequently learned that this was the three-part plan developed by Jim Knoll and contained the names of those involved at that time). According to John, it was at this time that Eve realized that a concerted effort was being made to unseat her and her cohorts and she feared that they would be successful. Nevertheless Eve had then bragged to John that, if this financial drain continued downward, she might just bring the whole district down with her. I was appalled. But, this did sound like Eve—she was being bull-headed—unable to admit that she had been wrong about the clinic and not willing to change course. The briefcase was eventually returned to the person who had lost it, who was one of our group. We were then aware that Eve knew of our plan, which was perhaps good. It might even influence her future actions in a more favorable direction.

John further explained that he previously had had a close working relationship with Eve, which had included devoting considerable time in the spring, working with her on developing the financial model for the new clinic. The time spent had caused him to fall behind in keeping up-to-date with the district's finances. This had worried him. He brought this to the attention of both Eve and the district's treasurer, Wayne Wilson, and both said for him to concentrate on the clinic plan and to catch up on the financial reports later. Only recently had he caught up, except for the unpaid bills with which Eve had just surprised him. He took considerable credit for the financial model that had been developed to support the new clinic plan and, furthermore, John felt that the strategy would have been successful if it had been implemented as structured. However, Eve had hired two *locum* physicians instead of the one recommended by Bob Bohlman, and she had augmented the plan to include night and weekend coverage which was a further expense. I suspect she wanted to show everyone that she could take this part of JR's plan for 24/7 coverage and give the community a completely operational clinic, disregarding the cost and the board's concurrence. I thought it was egomaniacal of her to think that she could disregard the original plan with its tight budget and still have it succeed. The main fallacy of her expanded plan was the lack of enough income-producing patients, this dearth likely to be the case for the foreseeable future.

John's next words shocked me and still surprise me to this day. "Do you want to know why Eve closed the clinic?" he asked. It isn't often that one is offered an answer to a major quandary that has been cogitating in one's mind, particularly when it is unexpected like this. All I could say was, "Yes, why?"

As John explained it, when Eve first came to Pagosa in February 2002 to become the district manager, she had tried to make friends with the clinic personnel, but with little success. The animosity seen now had been developing between her and the employees during the year. I thought it surprising that she didn't recognize that she couldn't have it both ways, to harass the employees and expect friendship at the same time. At Christmas of that year, 2002, Eve had told John that the clinic was having a Christmas party. She had not been invited; however, she was going to go anyway. She was going to hand out Christmas bonuses at the party. The employees were aware that they were getting bonuses, so that, in itself, would be no surprise. Apparently, Eve believed that by giving them their bonuses at the party personally she would somehow endear herself to them. John tried to dissuade her, saying he thought it was a bad idea, but to no avail.

Later, after the party, Eve told John that the party had been a disaster. None of the clinic employees had been friendly, not even after she had handed out their bonuses. She boldly assured John that she would get even. Thereafter, her relationship with the clinic employees, including the docs, deteriorated even more rapidly. John felt that it had become Eve's intent to make the clinic staff's lives so miserable that they would be driven to the action they had taken: resignation. As was happening too frequently these days, I was appalled by this disclosure.

I felt as if I was watching a tragic comedy. We were all being manipulated like puppets on a string, but who was the puppeteer? Eve? She manipulated, but was in turn a victim of her own desires and emotions that overrode rational judgment and decision-making. The stress on her must have been tremendous. I concluded that she was so overwhelmed by the situation in which she had immersed herself that now, seeing no way out, she was going to let events run their course to whatever end might result. This was very sad, not just for her but for all of us. I felt obligated, more than ever, to see that she did not "bring the entire district down."

I felt a pang of sympathy for Eve, having to go to this length, the Christmas party, to seek friendship. It is unfortunate that no one had seen her purpose in crashing the party and the great effort that it must have taken to walk into the "enemy camp." But then the strained relationship had already been established. However, a little understanding and friendship on the part of the staff might have averted the clinic crisis and changed the course of events.

I had to decide what to do with John's information. Though I had little reason to doubt John, I needed to verify that our financial situation was as bad as he claimed and that it was deteriorating as rapidly as he implied. One resource would be to look at the general ledger (GL). Because the Dr. Mary Fisher Clinic was a public entity, all records were available to anyone for the asking. In any case, as a board director, I should have immediate access to this information. Beyond that, I could not accomplish anything by myself. I would need help.

It didn't make sense to check out this information with Eve or Wally, as they were obviously already hiding it from board members—at least from the minority, Ken and me. Further, they would want to know the source of my information. If they found out that John had come to me with this information, I had no doubt that he would be fired. I decided that I needed a second opinion before taking any action. It was time to have another lunch with Jim at the DQ.

We met the next day. At this time our DQ was CC's, a deli where we could sit outside on nice days in the Pagosa sun. Jim usually ordered a beef barbecue sandwich with a Coke, and I usually had a meat loaf sandwich with root beer. We were both pretty well set in our ways, not only in our eating habits, but as well in our loyalty to the DQ.

I related John's story to Jim. He wasn't surprised at either part of the account, the financial situation or the Christmas tale. He felt that both were in Eve's character. I explained how I felt bound by my board oath to try to do something about the looming financial crisis, and the only way I could see this being accomplished was to have Eve removed from office. Jim was dubious that this could be accomplished, since she had the majority of the board behind her. He felt, as he had stated previously, that no major change could be accomplished until the next election, which was still some eight months away.

We talked further. I then outlined a plan to Jim that had been building in my mind. We knew that one board member, Ken, thought as we did. This left two board members who would have to be swayed to our side to get a majority vote. I thought that the best person to start with would be Wayne Wilson. As our treasurer, he was responsible for seeing that we maintained financial integrity. Who better to determine the state of our finances? If he saw a sufficiently worsening financial situation, I felt sure he would want to take some action. If we could persuade him to our way of thinking, then perhaps he would be the best person to persuade a fourth person to join us to give us a board majority. To my way of thinking, Laura seemed like the next most likely board member to see things our way.

Jim thought this was about the best approach we could come up with, and though he had doubts that it would be successful, he supported my taking this action.

I called John to apprise him of this plan. I wanted him to come along with me and tell his story to Wayne. This would make a much stronger case than if I relayed John's story to Wayne myself. John was hesitant; this would put him in jeopardy of losing his job. However, he realized that in having told me the story, I was bound to take some action, and whatever I did would likely place him jeopardy. John agreed to meet with Wayne.

I called Wayne to set up the appointment, telling him that I had an important district issue I wanted to discuss with him. I did not tell Wayne that I was bringing John along because I thought he might call either Eve or Wally to see what was going on.

We met in Wayne's office the next day. Surprise showed on Wayne's face when he saw John accompanying me. I explained to Wayne that John had come to me with a disturbing story about our finances, and as treasurer, I thought he should hear it first-hand. John then related the same account that he had told me. He left out the Christmas party tale. I felt this wasn't pertinent to the present situation and might just confuse the financial matter. Wayne appeared just as disturbed as I had been, and he queried John for further financial details.

I then jumped in to suggest what we might do to remedy the situation. I pointed out to Wayne that Eve had failed to follow the clinic plan with its tight budget. Just the opposite, she was pursuing an extravagant course by hiring an extra physician as well as instituting nighttime, 24/7 coverage. She was disregarding the plan approved by the board for the new clinic. As I saw it, this was the major cause of our rapidly deteriorating financial situation. Furthermore, as John had indicated, it was clear that she was unwilling to change direction. I said that I felt that our only recourse was to discharge Eve and hire a new administrator or, at the least, bring this matter before the board for discussion. I asked that Wayne join Ken and me in taking this action. Incidentally, I had relayed all this information to Ken beforehand, so I knew he was in agreement with this strategy. Of course, we would have to get one other board member to join us. I suggested to Wayne that Laura might be the best choice to join us, and I suggested that he might be the best person to contact her.

It was clear that Wayne was disturbed by all this new information. He said that he would have to think about it and that he would get back to me. I asked if he could think of any other course of action that we might take. He could not come up with any other idea, at least not at this time.

Afterwards, both John and I felt somewhat encouraged by Wayne's response. However, I realized the predicament now facing Wayne: his financial responsibility as treasurer versus his prior record of having virtually backed all of this administration's prior decisions. If we had weighed these two factors beforehand, perhaps we could have predicted the outcome. However, at this time I saw no alternative. For better or worse, the die was cast once more.

CHAPTER 12

A DECISION GONE WRONG

In any moment of decision, the best thing you can do is the right thing, the next best thing is the wrong thing, and the worst thing you can do is nothing.
- Theodore Roosevelt

Several hours before the scheduled board meeting, Wayne called. I held my breath. He had thought about what John had told him and what I had suggested as a course of action.

"I didn't know what to do," he said, "so I went to Eve and Wally and told them the whole story."

I grimaced and could actually feel my heart palpitate.

"What are they going to do?" I asked.

He didn't know. They had not told him.

I was flabbergasted and did not know what to say. I thanked Wayne for calling and hung up.

The board was meeting in just a few hours. What course of action could I take beforehand? Even though Jim had doubts about what I had proposed, he had supported me. I called him and told him what had transpired. In his usual calm manner, he gave me some reassuring words of support. I can recall just feeling numb about the whole affair. Also, I knew that poor John would bear the brunt of what had now turned into a fiasco.

I ran into Ken just before the meeting started. Wayne had called him, too, and told him about going to Eve and Wally and telling them the whole story. Wayne didn't know whether he had done the right thing or not, so he was going to resign from the board. My immediate thought was that he should not resign but should stay on board to check on our finances. Both he and John were CPA's. What better team could we have in determining whether or not a financial crisis was actually pending? I understood Wayne's quandary but not his decision to quit. Wayne's staying and support could have given John some protection as well. After all, as far as Eve and Wally knew, this whole matter was still in-house.

Neither Wayne nor John attended the board meeting. John always gave the financial report, so I assumed that either Eve or Wally had spoken to him about this matter. This would explain his absence. Eve did not indicate why John was absent, but said only that there was no financial report because it had not been completed.

It was clear that my actions were going to get John fired, but in retrospect I do not know what other course I could have taken. I suppose I could have brought the whole affair up at a board meeting, but then John's part would have come out anyway and he would have been in the same predicament. The majority of the board being in Eve's "pocket" made it likely that the board would not have taken any action.

On the other hand, the information would have been made public, and perhaps a public outcry would have forced the board to take some action. But because the board had repeatedly ignored previous public outcries, I realized they likely would have done nothing.

The poorest option would have been to have ignored the situation, a course that I could not responsibly have taken.

After the meeting, I learned that John had been placed on administrative leave with pay, pending an investigation into "certain financial matters."

However, this was not the only major problem to arise at the October board meeting. I need to digress to provide some background about events that had occurred earlier in the month.

CHAPTER 13

TRUTH OR CONSEQUENCES

The board members had been told at the two previous board meetings that the final consultative EMS report had not been received, just a preliminary report. Eve was not going to release any information until the final report was in hand. However, a number of us had heard rumors that the final report had actually been received. I decided to call Allan Hughes, the EMS consultant who had performed the study, now some three months ago, and ask about the status of his report.

I put in a call to Allan, reached him immediately, and asked about the EMS report.

He said that he had sent ten copies of the final document to the district manager, Eve Hegarty, on September 8, 2003, a month and a half before, by certified mail, and he had received a receipt, in turn, indicating that the district had accepted the report on September 10. Before sending the "final" report, Eve had asked for changes to it and also for further consultation on the EMS, but there had subsequently been no further contact so he had assumed his work was completed.

I asked him what possible reason they could have for denying having received the final report.

Allan said that the report reflected poorly on the administration to the point that he thought the EMS was in a near-crisis mode. They probably would be embarrassed to make the report public.

I asked Allan to email me a copy of the report.

He said he would do so and also send a copy of the receipt showing that Eve had received the report. Further, Allan indicated that he had been paid in full, which he felt supported the fact that he had completed his work and that he had, indeed, sent the "Final Report."

The EMS consultative report arrived by email the next day. I had known the EMS was in trouble, but this document indicated that things were even worse than I had suspected. Previously, Kathy, the EMS ops manager, had called me on several occasions to tell me of their predicament and her fear that Eve was going to fire her at any time. As she had told me before, she felt the only thing holding Eve back was her fear that the EMT's would quit en masse if she was fired.

I called Kathy now to discuss the report. She said that Eve had shown her the EMS report back in September, over a month ago, and had made her promise not to tell anyone about it. The report detailed how Eve interfered with the everyday management of the EMS. It stated that insufficient financial data had been provided to adequately assess that area. It concluded by saying that the EMS was in a near-crisis mode and that the morale of the EMT's was exceedingly low.

It was time for another lunch with Jim at the DQ.

Jim was appalled by the EMS report but not surprised, having been aware of the difficulties at EMS, too. We agreed that there wasn't much we could do other than support Kathy and the EMT's as much as possible.

We then discussed what should be done with the report itself. Both Eve and Wally had misled the board and the public about not having received this document, claiming that just a preliminary report had been received. If I went to Eve or Wally alone, I knew they would try to diffuse the situation, either by ignoring it or trying to minimize its serious nature. I felt that they needed an awakening;,something to startle them into realizing how the general public perceived them—secretive and not truthful. This lack of professionalism had to stop. I thought the document must be made public. I told Jim that I wanted to present the EMS report at the next board meeting, not only to the board but to the public as well. He agreed that under the circumstances that would be the correct thing to do.

One thing I didn't understand. What was Eve thinking when she requested the EMS consultation in the first place? She had known the EMS was in serious trouble or else she wouldn't have requested the evaluation. It is hard to believe that she didn't have some insight into the source of the problem. But then it appeared that Eve had little understanding at all of why the employees were unhappy. Later I heard that Eve had requested the consultation believing that it would be solely for in-house use and not for public consumption. However, she had announced she was obtaining the evaluation and the employees were aware of the consultants' visit, so there was little chance of keeping the report quiet and exclusively for her own use. Anyway, the report didn't really tell us anything that we didn't already suspect; it just confirmed our suspicions. It would have been better to have just released the report when it was received and state to the public that measures were being taken to correct the situation. As it turned out, Eve actually had already instituted some of the recommendations in the report. I will never understand her reasoning for keeping the report secret. It made no sense.

Returning to the October board meeting, the budget for the upcoming year was next on the agenda. It appeared to be a template of the previous year's budget. What stood out was the number of patients expected to be seen at the clinic in the coming year. This number was comparable to the previous year when the "old clinic" with its full complement of physicians and bevy of patients was in operation. I pointed this out, indicating that this was an impossible number with so many of the patients having left to follow their docs to their new locations. The current patient figures, using the *locum* docs, were quite low, and there was little reason to expect this much improvement in the coming year. Efforts to find new full-time docs who would reside in the community had been unsuccessful so far. Eve said she felt that they would be able to find and hire new, full-time docs soon and that the budget was therefore realistic.

Having made my point, I didn't pursue the matter further.

The last order of business was opening the session up for queries from the audience. We weren't using Robert's Rules of Order any longer, but rather "Wally's Rules," which said that each audience member had two minutes to ask a question or make a comment. Wally was using this mechanism to control crowd participation, particularly after the last meeting which had mimicked a "bar room brawl." Laura had brought a clock along and was to time each person asking a question or making a comment. I was embarrassed to be a part of this sophomoric antic.

J.R. rose and asked if the final EMS consultative report had been received. Eve said it had not, just the preliminary report as she had stated the month before. J.R. followed up saying that he had heard that the report had been received. Eve repeated her denial.

This was my opportunity. I could feel my heart pounding. I jumped up and said loudly, "That's not true." I picked up my briefcase from the floor and slammed it on the table in front of me. I flipped open the cover and took out a sheaf of copies of the final EMS report. Striding around the table passing out the report to each shocked board member, I said, "Here is the Final Report." Of course, I handed a copy to Eve. I then made sure that the reporter from the *Pagosa Springs Sun*, who was sitting in the audience, got a copy. I handed a copy to J.R., who had first requested the report. The audience seemed stunned.

I sat down. I then related that I had called Allan Hughes recently to ask why we hadn't received the final EMS consultative report. He had expressed his surprise, indicating that he had sent ten copies of the final report on September 8th by certified mail and in return had received a receipt saying the reports had been received and accepted on September 10th. In addition, he had been paid in full for his services. I didn't state that Eve and Wally had been untruthful again, as I thought this was now obvious to everyone.

Both the board and the audience still appeared stunned.

I have to give Eve credit because she then made a vain attempt to diffuse my performance. She said that this was still just the preliminary report and not the Final Report. To me, and I'm sure to the audience, this was ludicrous. Her attempt to cover up was transparent to everyone. The meeting was adjourned shortly thereafter without any further queries or discussion. As the crowd dispersed, there was a loud buzz of conversation about what had just transpired.

CHAPTER 14

REVERBERATIONS

We were to go into executive session immediately after the board meeting to discuss a personnel matter. By law, the audience could not participate in this session so we had to wait for the room to clear. As soon as the board meeting ended, before all the members of the public had filed out, Wally began berating me, obviously for embarrassing him and Eve in public. I reminded him that it was he and Eve who had lied to the board and the public about the report. Wally then claimed that he had never lied in his life. I then reminded him that he had also lied on the résumé that he had submitted to the board when applying for the director position, where he claimed, "I have 25+ years experience in hospital and clinic administration...." This infuriated him further, and his tone and volume escalated. I decided to leave the room and go out into the hall and talk to friends congregated there until the executive session would begin.

As I was walking out of the room, I heard Wally say, "F--- bastard." There was no doubt but that he was referring to me. At first, I couldn't believe my ears, but then I realized that Wally had been terribly embarrassed by the actual truth coming out about the EMS report. Both he and Eve had been caught as prevaricators before the public. I have mentioned previously that Wally frequently tried to intimidate me at board meetings.

Perhaps I had reached a breaking point. I thought that Wally should get some of his own medicine so I turned and walked back into the room. Only Eve and some the board members were present now. They were all on the far side of the table. I pointed a finger at Wally's nose and said, "Wally, you are an a--hole."

The others appeared aghast at my out-of-character charge, but Wally just had a smug expression on his face as if I were doing exactly what he wanted.

I then pointed to his abdomen and said, "But then you don't have one so you can't be an a--hole." Wally previously had had surgery for colon cancer. With that I turned and stalked out of the room. I knew immediately that this was a mistake and unprofessional. I suppose I had had it.

After talking to some friends in the hall for a few minutes, I returned to the conference room. The executive session was just getting underway. I retook my seat next to Wally and immediately broke in, "I want to apologize for the remarks that I just made to Wally." Wally said nothing, neither apologizing nor mentioning his profanity towards me.

The meeting continued without any further mention of this incident or of the final report. In fact, the purpose of the meeting was forgotten; we never discussed the personnel matter for which the meeting was called. We discussed a few minor issues and then adjourned. I left immediately, not wanting to discuss anything with anyone.

Afterwards, I reflected on the happenings of that evening. I thought that some would say that I had gone overboard in presenting the final report. I suppose you could say this usually quiet doc had been playing to the crowd. On the other hand, if Eve and Wally had learned anything, I thought that they would be very careful not to misinform the board or the public in the future. As the passage of time would show, they had learned nothing.

On Thursday our newspaper, The *Pagosa Springs Sun*, reported on the board meeting and the EMS consultative report, so it got the attention I thought it deserved.

I knew from talking to people in town that more and more people were becoming aware of the shenanigans of Eve and Wally and their supporting board members. They, in turn, appeared oblivious of this fact and seemed to think the majority of the populace was behind them. They had mentioned more than once that they thought that the meetings were packed with my and Norm Vance's cronies, and this was why the audience was always against them. Why they didn't have supporters of their own at the meetings apparently hadn't crossed their minds. I have to say that many people whom I had never met would come up to me after our meetings and say they appreciated what I was doing for them. Both my wife and I received many phone calls and emails thanking "Dr. Blide." Of the hundreds that I talked to after these meetings and elsewhere during the year, I can only recall one or two who criticized me. The support bolstered me and gave me confidence that what I was doing was right.

I met Jim for lunch at the DQ several days later. He had been at the board meeting and so was aware of my presentation of the final EMS report. However, he was not aware of the incident between the two meetings. I related the exchange with Wally. At first Jim laughed. Then turning more serious, he said that I shouldn't have lost my cool. I told him I thought I had remained calm and collected, and that my actions and words had been reasonable. He gave me a dubious look. Furthermore, I said I thought that Wally had it coming. He agreed with that assessment but said it was still unwise. I assented to that, and we let it go.

We talked about the final EMS report and whether their lying would have any impact on the other board members. We thought not. In fact, we thought it likely that board members Betty and Laura, and probably Martha, too, had known about the final report and, by never speaking up, had covertly participated in the cover up.

We did think that with the election being not far off, people would remember and this would most likely influence their vote. That, of course, had been one purpose for making the EMS report public at the board meeting in front of a large audience—an untruth has its consequences.

CHAPTER 15

PETTY OBSTINACY

Soon after the board meeting I called Eve at her office and requested a copy of the general ledger (GL). At times these people really made me shake my head in disbelief, to wit, Eve said that it would take too much paper as well as take all day for someone to do the copying. I said, "Put it on a CD," inasmuch as the GL was in the computer. Eve said that the GL wasn't up-to-date and it couldn't be released until it was complete. I realized then that they weren't going to give up the GL without a fight. What petty infighting! I resolved to use legal means to get the GL if necessary.

The next day I called our district's attorney in Denver and explained that management was denying me access to the GL. He was sympathetic and said that he would both email and send a "snail mail" letter to Eve and Wally explaining that the general ledger was a public document and that they had to release it to me and to anyone else who requested to see it.

A week later I called the district office to let them know I was stopping by to pick up a copy of the GL. By this time, I was sure that they had at least received the email from our district's attorney. As I suspected, they had not made a copy of the GL, yet but they did give me a date and time to stop in and pick it up.

There was so much animosity by Eve and Wally toward me at this time that a friend suggested I bring a witness with me to the district office. He didn't think it safe to go in there alone. As it turned out, this was perceptive advice. Dick Babillis, the former board chairman, and I had become good friends, so I asked him to accompany me to pick up the GL.

On entering the district's office, Dick and I saw that Wally was present. Had Eve asked him to be present to give her moral support? Immediately sensing an air of hostility, I was glad I had asked Dick to accompany me.

I requested the record. Eve asked why Dick Babillis was there. I said I had asked him to accompany me. She then accused me of wanting to show the GL to Dick, in which circumstance she wasn't going to give me the record. I presumed that our district's attorney had notified her that the GL was a public document, as he had said he would do, and so available to anyone upon request, something she was now ignoring. Eve was right in my face, yelling, as if challenging me to back off or do something worse. All I could see and feel was pure rage. Wally just stood in the background with a smug expression on his face. I asked again, "May I have the GL?"

"No," she said.

I could see nothing was going to be gained by remaining, so I turned to Dick and said, "Let's go," and we walked out.

Outside, Dick just shook his head in disbelief. I thanked him for his help. I truly believe that had I gone in there alone, they would have fabricated some unseemly story about me—or worse.

CHAPTER 16

A WELCOME REPRIEVE

In early November, the board went on a retreat to Durango to do some strategic planning. To my knowledge no such endeavor had been undertaken in recent years. This certainly seemed like a good idea, and I heartily supported it.

The purpose of the retreat was several-fold. First, the board would create a new mission statement, then a set of values, and, thirdly, a vision for the future, both near- and long-term. A committee of the board would then hold a series of meetings with various community groups and leaders to get their input on our health care needs, both present and future.

Eve hired an experienced leader, who did an excellent job. As it turned out, this was undoubtedly the best meeting held by the board during this tumultuous year. Everyone contributed, there was no rancor, and we bounced ideas off one another. It was actually a pleasant experience, particularly after our last two raucous board meetings back in Pagosa.

Initially we revised our old mission statement, broadening it, essentially saying that we would promote the best healthcare program possible in a fiscally responsible manner for all individuals, be they rich or poor, in our three county areas. We then created a set of values to which the board members would adhere: honesty, integrity, truthfulness, responsibility, and accountability. It made me wonder, since some of these values had been violated by some of us as recently as the past week. Were these individuals aware of this dichotomy? Or perhaps were we seeing a rebirth, a new beginning?

In setting our near-term goals, two thoughts were paramount: to establish better relations with the public and to establish better relations with the local docs. The words were easy to say, but what actions would be taken to make this happen? The idea of meeting with groups of citizens to get their input in planning for the future, particularly the communication part, would be an excellent start. However, our relations with the public were largely determined by what went on at the monthly board meetings, and what transpired at these sessions was widely publicized. Wally's adversarial position was well known, there being no better description of this relationship than what appeared in the paper earlier in the fall describing our meetings as, "A circus without the cotton candy and elephants...." Until Wally's behavior could be brought under control, other efforts would be useless. I could have brought this up at the meeting, but I did not. I was sure it would cause turmoil, and I didn't want to destroy our newly-found amicable relationship.

Our longer-term vision included expanding the clinic to include further services, such as enlarging our radiology area to include a CT scanning machine to be shared by all physicians in town. Another was to bring in more out-of-town specialists to see patients locally, negating patients' need to leave town for these services.

Betty suggested providing an obstetric service by either getting an obstetrician to open a local practice or by bringing in a midwife. I knew we were too small a community to attract an obstetrician, even part-time, but a midwife might be a possibility. The problem here was that, if a complication or emergency occurred during birth, the birthing mother and baby would have to be transported to Durango, some 60 miles away, not something to look forward to. On the other hand, I recalled hearing, while in Telluride, that they had two midwives working in town and their nearest hospital and obstetrician were some 65 miles away. I voiced these thoughts.

Betty also mentioned that we should consider having a hospital some time in the future. In fact, she mentioned that she had talked to a director of a critical access hospital up north to gather information. At this time this was just a distant thought.

Another thought was to develop a closer relationship with Mercy Hospital, particularly with their emergency department, in view of the recent critical EMS consultative report.

Toward the end of the day I began thinking that we had an abundance of good ideas. This was a good start, but I saw an immediate problem: implementation of most of these ideas.

For example, Eve asked if I would contact the local docs about setting up a series of meetings so we could begin a dialogue to improve the relations between our groups. I agreed, though I already foresaw the outcome of such an effort. I did contact Dr. Jim Pruitt afterwards and queried him about such a get-together. He categorically refused, saying that he would have nothing to do with the board while Eve and Wally were still in charge. This was the answer I had expected, and I relayed the reply to Eve.

Of course, many of our ideas for the future required the cooperation of the local physicians. Knowing that Jim spoke for the other physicians, I did not need to check with them. My recent trip to Mercy had also answered the question about developing a closer relationship with them. I knew nothing was going to happen until we had a different leadership. How could a healthcare entity expect to develop and grow without the cooperation of the medical community? The short-sighted vision and particularly the words and actions of the leadership of the district were now coming home to roost.

At the end of the meeting, Eve came up to me and said that she and Wally wanted to speak with me privately for a moment. We went into the room next door. Eve said that she and Wally wanted to end the animosity that had developed between us. Could we shake hands and start over as friends. I am the last person to refuse a friendship, even after all that had transpired in the last few months. I said, "Of course, let's be friends," and I meant it. Wally shook my hand and Eve gave me a big hug. Eve could be a very charming person when she wanted to be.

Patti and I lived on the same road as the two clinics. I would drive by our public clinic several times a day, going back and forth to town. When the "old" clinic was operating, I would count 12-to-15 cars in the parking lot at a time. Now, with the new clinic, I would count five or six cars. This pretty

The Family Medicine Clinic

well represented the decrease in patient traffic. The private Family Medicine Clinic next door almost always had a full parking lot of 20+ cars.

I mentioned the "car count" at one of our board meetings, and thereafter I saw that the employees, who had previously parked in back, began parking in front. Obviously, they were trying to make it look like we were seeing more patients.

Our public clinic now had two *locum* docs and a nurse practitioner. They took turns, only one professional on duty at a time. One MD covered three days a week, the nurse practitioner worked one day, and the other MD covering three days including a clinic day on Saturday. All participated in off-site coverage for Sunday and nights. After-hours business was nil. Our medical director mentioned that he had been called into the clinic at night only once in three months. This was a good arrangement for giving full coverage, but hardly worth either the effort or the cost. We couldn't afford it and were going further into debt each month. Even at this late date it might not have been too late to cut back to one *locum* doc and the nurse practitioner, plus eliminating the night and weekend coverage, which would have decreased expenses quite significantly. After all, this had been the original plan presented by Bob Bohlman and approved by the board. I couldn't imagine Eve considering this retrenchment, so I never mentioned it. Another confrontation wouldn't have accomplished anything worthwhile.

I always made it a point to say hello to the *locum* physician, who was the current medical director of our clinic and always attended the board meetings to give the monthly clinic report. I sympathized with him because he took flack from the local physicians, with whom he was in competition, as well as from some in the community who looked on him as being a part of Eve's group. He tried to stay apolitical and handled the situation well. I admired his efforts to balance himself between the public and the administration.

In late fall, Dr. Jim Knoll persuaded Dr. Jim Pruitt, the head of Family Medicine, to run for a board seat in the spring election. We felt this was a coup for us and the community. If Dr. Pruitt and I were elected, it would give us two MD's on the board. We realized that Pruitt's practice would always come first and that was as it should be. Jim had practiced in Pagosa for over 20 years and no one knew the history of healthcare in the district better than he did. In the past he had had chances to join the district in practicing medicine, but he had deferred, always preferring the private practice of medicine. His way was the more difficult, both in terms of finances and the time spent working, but he could maintain his independence and call his own shots. All he had to do was look at the recent events with our public clinic to see that in the past he had made the right choice. On the other hand, if he had been actively involved with the district, perhaps the recent events and the closing of the clinic would not have occurred. Dr. Jim Pruitt was strong in many ways—for sure, no one would have pushed him around.

With ruddy good looks and wavy red hair, Dr. Pruitt in many ways exemplified the character of "the old country doctor"—caring, hard-working and dedicated to his profession. One could see the pride he took in his accomplishments, his clinic, and his thriving practice. He said once that it had been his goal to practice medicine in a small, rural, mountain town, to give of his talents and at the same time to be able to enjoy the outdoors.

Jim Pruitt had a partner, John Picarro, an intense, knowledgeable young doc with craggy good looks dominated by wavy black hair and beard. New to the clinic two years ago he likened their practice to a "MASH" unit, similar to the medical battlefield groups set up during the Korean War and exemplified by the TV show by the same name. They always had a full waiting room and always had a flurry of activity in the common area outside the exam rooms. More than once, I stood there and admired their practice as I observed the docs and staff interacting so smoothly.

CHAPTER 17

DESPERATE CHARGES

At the beginning of the November board meeting Eve announced that John, our finance officer, had been fired because of incompetence. The reason given: they had found "errors" in the books going back to the beginning of the year. A few of us knew that this was not likely to be true;. However, there was little we could do about it now. No mention was made about John coming to me with his worries about our financial situation, which was obviously the actual cause of his discharge.

I thought of saying something in support of John at the board meeting, but I knew I would have to back it up with objective evidence to counter Eve's accusation. I did not have that proof, and I did not have any way of getting it. Perhaps I should have brought the whole story out into the open—John coming to me with his fear of a looming financial crisis—but that would not have saved John his job. There were too many negatives for pursuing this course of action, so I said nothing. If I had, it would have raised quite a hullabaloo, and this fall had already seen its share of theatrics.

Several days later I ran into John and expressed my sympathy. He was rather blasé about the whole affair. As he had indicated previously, he had known what he was getting into and the risks involved. He had been a staunch supporter of Eve, but when he saw her going astray, as financial officer he had felt obliged to try to correct the situation. John was a good person, he had done the right thing, and I admired his professionalism. I just wish that things had turned out differently.

When I asked John what he would be doing now, he said he had always wanted to visit the "Keys" and felt this was a good time to go. He thought he would open an accounting practice upon his return, as well as continue with his part-time practice as a massage therapist. I wished him well.

Other business at the November board meeting included approval of the budget for 2004. No changes had been made, and the budget was as unrealistic as before. It was too late to develop an alternative budget, since the deadline for submitting the budget to the state was upon us. In any case, Eve had the support of the board so the budget was going to pass whether I voted yea or nay. Budgets could always be revised at a later date. I voted affirmative. I did not want to appear to be an obstructionist, particularly when it would not make a difference.

Our treasurer, Wayne Wilson, following through on his earlier decision to resign, submitted his letter of resignation at the meeting. Perhaps I should have tried to talk Wayne out of resigning, but I felt no strong urge to do so.

Before the meeting ended, Laura made a motion to cancel our December board meeting because of Christmas. Although I objected, this passed. I felt that we had important matters to discuss, particularly our precarious financial status. For the third month in a row we had no financial report. Laura was our new treasurer, and it now fell on her shoulders to see that these reports were brought up to date. Eve had an MBA and should have been able to do the monthly reports herself. At the least, we should have hired an accountant or bookkeeper by now to do the books. On the other hand, perhaps we had no report because they didn't want to show the desperation in our financial situation. The worst would be that no one knew our financial status because the records hadn't been updated since John had been placed on administrative leave. I suspected that Eve had created a monster that was now running out of control.

After the board meeting, we went into executive session to review Eve's contract. But first, Eve wanted the floor. She said that she was bringing grievances to the board about my interfering in two administrative matters. I was dumbfounded. While glaring at me, she accused me of going over her head when Kathy had fired the EMT back in October. I thought this was absurd. I explained that Kathy had said that both Eve and Wally were out of town and she had to take immediate action, so I had agreed to help out. Of course, Kathy had the ulterior motive of setting me up to see John at that time which I did not mention. I was sure Eve was just trying to embarrass me, a rather desperate effort.

The other affair was even more ludicrous. One of the female EMT's, Terry Clifford, had a worker's compensation claim against the district for a work-related injury. She had asked me to testify on her behalf, and she had put my name on the papers she had submitted to Worker's Comp. I had called Terry to explain that I could not help her for two reasons: I had no knowledge of the injury, and as a board member I was legally bound not to testify against the district. Eve was not aware of my conversation with Terry. Otherwise she would not have brought the matter up. These complaints died here. So much for our new-found friendship, sealed with a hug and a handshake, which was only a few weeks old. This led me to surmise that this "friendship" was probably founded on the hope that I would be able to bring the docs to the table to heal the schism between the two parties. When this foundered, so did our new friendship.

Getting back to the original reason for the executive session, Wally indicated that they wanted to redo Eve's contract to include a raise of 5 percent. I was shocked. Now it was my turn. Fixing my gaze on Eve, I said that her performance in the past six months hardly warranted an increase in salary. I further indicated that I was amazed that anyone would even entertain such an idea. Ken mirrored my view. He made his disdain for this recommendation apparent by arising abruptly and walking out of the meeting. I mirrored Ken's action and with a look of disdain arose and walked out as well. Neither of us wanted to dignify even voting nay for what we knew was an absurd consideration. Of course, the motion was made and passed by the remaining board members, who always supported Eve, and the new contract went into effect.

In early December I was told that Martha, our board secretary, had resigned. The rumor making the rounds was that her superiors at work had told her that the health district had become too politicized and that she would either have to quit the board or else they would have to let her go. I believe she was a state employee, but I did not know the nature of her work. She was the quietest of the board members and rarely said anything. As our secretary, I felt she had done a good job with the exception that she always supported Eve without good reason, seemingly without weighing the facts.

Early in the month I again called the district office, saying I was coming in to pick up the general ledger. This time they were agreeable and said a copy would be waiting. Again, I brought Dick Babillis with me. No way was I going in there without a chaperone/witness. On this occasion, as Dick and I entered the office, we were handed a copy of the general ledger. We immediately turned and left without a word being exchanged.

On looking over the GL, it became clear that John's worst fears were fact.

Although we had a little money in the bank, it was apparent that there was a huge backlog of unpaid bills. We had to have at least sufficient funds to meet our biweekly salaries. How long would our creditors wait to be paid? No tax money would be available until March, so we had to survive three more months somehow. I didn't have an answer to these questions, and I didn't believe that anyone else did, either. We did have income from the clinic and EMS patients, and though both services ran a deficit, hopefully this would be enough to cover the employees' salaries. Clearly it wouldn't be enough to keep our burgeoning debt from growing larger.

COUNTERPOINT

A meeting most likely took place between Eve and Wally after the October board meeting where the EMS final report was revealed and the altercation occurred between Wally and Dick (speculation that a meeting took place with the subsequent discussion):

Eve, angrily, "That troublemaker, Dick, handing out that EMS report at the board meeting. I could have choked him. Wally, do you think we should do something to smooth the waters?"

"It's out! We shouldn't do or say anything. It would just add fuel to the fire. It's best to just let it be. People will forget. But, Eve, I think we can make something of the affair that occurred between the board meeting and the executive session. I was trying to goad Dick into reacting to my taunting and I finally got him to respond. I really got him mad. Did you see him come back and swear at me? Then he tweaked my nose and poked me in the abdomen."

"Wally, I heard what he said. I saw him point at you, but I was in the back and that's all I saw."

"He hit me. He broke my colostomy bag. The contents ran down my leg and smelled up the place."

"He actually touched you?" queried Eve.

"He did, don't you believe me?"

"Wally, if you say so, I believe you."

"Eve, I'm thinking of calling the police and charging Dick with assault. That could more than nullify any benefit Dick got from revealing the EMS report. The election isn't that far away. If we can get him charged, and he is found guilty, it would really make him look bad. It would reflect badly on Jim Knoll and their cronies, too. I think we may have been handed a gift horse, and we need to take advantage of it."

"Wally, did he really strike you that hard that it broke your bag? I can't say that I really smelled anything in the executive session."

"I said it happened, you have to believe me."

"I do, Wally. I think we need to check with Betty and Laura before you go to the police. We need to find out what they saw and heard. They were the only others there. Ken was out of the room, so it was just the four of us—that should help. I'll set up a meeting with Betty and Laura."

A few days later a meeting with Eve, Wally, Betty and Laura present may have taken place.

"Gals, Eve and I have met and talked over the incident that happened at the October board meeting, Dick dumping the EMS Report on us. We have decided not to make any public comment about the report. It was bad and we should just let it go at that. People will forget.

"However, Eve and I have come up with an idea to balance out the embarrassment, which is why we are meeting. You will remember that between our two meetings, Dick came up and swore at me, twisted my nose and then poked me in the abdomen. He broke my colostomy bag and the contents ran down my leg and soiled my trousers. It smelled up the place, too. We need to know what you saw and heard. Laura?"

"Wally, I was sitting right there. I remember shouting, 'Stop it! Stop it!' and pounding the table."

"Did you see him strike me, Laura?"

"I was too upset, I don't know."

"He did, he twisted my nose. He hit me in the stomach and broke my bag. He did it on purpose. He was really mad. You have to believe me."

"Wally, if you say so, I believe you."

"What about you Betty, what did you see?"

"I don't know. It was terrible. I didn't think he would do that."

"Eve and I talked it over. We decided that, if we all agree on what happened, I'll go to the police and bring charges against Dick for assaulting me. With the election coming up in a few months it would really make Dick look bad. It would make their whole group look bad. It could really give us a boost with the voters at election time. OK, we all agree that Dick swore at me, tweaked my nose and struck me in the abdomen—broke my colostomy bag, soiling my trousers and smelling up the place.

"I think this is going to work, Eve. Do you have any last minute thoughts?"

"No, but I wonder what Dick will do. He is not going to take this sitting down."

"There was no one else there to disagree with us—fortunately."

No one could have predicted the outcome of this one-act play, certainly not the actors.

CHAPTER 18

FELEUX Á MANAGE
(CRAZINESS OF A GROUP)

In mid-December, when most of the world was thinking of Christmas and gifts, I received a present: the proverbial sack of coal. A letter from the county sheriff arrived, saying that Wally was accusing me of harassment and of assaulting him in October during the recess between the board meeting and the executive session. An enclosed statement of an interview with Wally said that without provocation I had sworn at him, "grabbed my nose and pulled" and "… just walked up and hit me with his palm, open-handed, and popped my seal (on his colostomy bag)." Furthermore, the liquid stool had run down his leg, soiling his trousers and producing a foul odor. At first I thought this must be hoax.

Accompanying the sheriff's letter were statements from interviews with Betty, Laura and Eve, all corroborating Wally's statement. I was aghast with disbelief. I hadn't even come close to touching Wally, let alone hitting him and breaking his colostomy bag. I had sat next to Wally on returning to the executive session, and I had not noticed either soiled trousers or a foul odor.

The detective requested that I call him and set up an appointment for an interview. I did so. Before I met with the detective, I wrote down my recollection of the whole affair. I thought it significant that, when I turned and retraced my steps back into the room to confront Wally, I was on the opposite side of the table, more than three feet from him. How then could I have reached that far across the table to grab his nose and strike him in the abdomen with the palm of my hand?

First, I went down to the Community Center conference room to check out the dimensions of the table which, as I thought, was 36 inches across. The only way I could have reached Wally would be if I had put one hand down in the middle of the table for support and had then stretched forward toward Wally. I did not do so. I thought the detective would see that I couldn't physically have assaulted Wally in determining whether or not this fiasco had actually occurred.

Wally's statement said that I was initially on the same side of the table when I struck him in the abdomen, and I then walked around the table and reached across and pulled on his nose. This could have been an Abbot and Costello routine if it were not so serious.

The detective was pleasant and non-committal during the interview, essentially just collecting the facts. I told him the occurrence of events and gave him my written statement. He said that the district attorney would get in touch with me to let me know whether or not they were going to prefer charges against me.

Later I listened to the CD containing the actual interviews with the accusers. It was enlightening to hear how these four described me, the disdain they felt. Never would I have imagined that I was so "hated" by this group, and that is not too strong a word to describe the feelings they evinced. Their frustration with me was palpable. In my view they had taken an unfortunate incident and had distorted it out of all proportion. Then, like a pack of coyotes catching a lone prey in the forest, they had set upon me.

The police investigator sought detailed information from each of the board members present as well as from the district manager, Eve Hegarty. They all agreed that I had verbally assaulted Wally, but they all denied that he had provoked me in any way, by calling me a name or otherwise. If their denials were true, it was remarkable that they could remember so many details but not one of them could remember Wally's tirade and then calling me a "f---ing bastard," which was what had triggered the affair. They all said that I had physically assaulted Wally, poking him in the abdomen, breaking his colostomy bag, and I grabbing and twisting his nose. They all said my blow had soiled Wally's trousers and had produced a foul odor. They differed on the course of events. Some had me on the same side of the table as Wally, some on the other side. Some had Wally going to the restroom, while Wally himself never mentioned it. There was little agreement other than the words that I had sworn and the claim that I had physically assaulted Wally. They iterated that Wally was defending himself before the event occurred, saying that he wasn't a liar and that he had never lied in his life. In response to this latter claim I had retorted that Wally had lied in the résumé he had submitted to the board in applying for a board position. Eve said that Wally had never said that he was a health care administrator, just that he had worked in hospital and clinic administration. Apparently this is what he had told Eve. I knew this to be untrue from the detective's report that I had obtained the summer before.

Not everyone present at this fiasco was recorded on the CD. Martha, Eve's friend and our board secretary who always voted with Betty, Laura and Wally, was not one of those interviewed. I had to presume that she did not agree with the charges and was not willing to participate with them in this fiction.

At this time I thought of the board's recent retreat in Durango, where we had developed a set of values for the board. Honesty and integrity were among those values that came to mind. What had happened? It appeared that the goal of this group of four was to win the coming election no matter the cost, including destroying my reputation—truly Machiavellian.

It was clear to me that this group had met in advance to make sure that their stories were in agreement. This was never clearer than from Betty's remark to the police that she had been waiting for this interview for a long time and had written down her recollection of the course of events. She mentioned that she was officially a victim's advocate. I wondered where her victim's advocacy had been when the employees were being persecuted, an apt description for how they had been treated.

After Christmas, I received a letter from the DA's office stating that formal charges were being brought against me and that I was to appear in court in February.

I had no doubt that Wally had hatched this plan to get back at me for embarrassing him and Eve in public over the final EMS report. I believe Wally persuaded the others to go along with him by implying that this would take me out of the election and also reflect badly on our group as a whole. To this day, I do not know what the others, Eve, Betty and Laura, actually saw at the encounter. I recall Laura sitting at the table, so perhaps she had a view. The others were standing in the back and to the side, so I doubt they could actually see whether or not I touched Wally. This was politics—dirty politics at that. It had never occurred to me when I volunteered to join the board that such a charade could happen. I had actually believed that we were all honorable people, sharing a heartfelt community project.

I saw that these charges posed a problem for me and for my fellow nominees in running for election. Until the charges were cleared, I could be under suspicion by the public, especially by those who did not know me. Although our justice system presumes one innocent until proven otherwise, this often is not so with the public. There might be doubt, and this could color people's opinions until the charges were cleared. Jim was right; my reaction to Wally's taunting had been a big mistake. I was realizing that in politics one had better always be cautious. I was learning this lesson the hard way. My worst fear was what effect this would have on my partners running for election.

It wasn't to be avoided. The *Pagosa Springs Sun* ran a short notice of the charges Wally was bringing against me at the bottom of the front page. I was mortified.

Because this whole affair was a farce, I had no doubt that the truth would come out and this hoax would be revealed to be just that. It was an effort, but I did not let this affair affect our Christmas spirit. Our daughter, son and grandkids visited. We skied, feasted and had a great time.

Earlier in the fall someone in town had complained to the Colorado State Health Department that they thought the new Dr. Mary Fisher Medical Center (the clinic) was being run improperly, and they feared that some practices might be endangering patient care. The source of the allegations was never revealed.

In early December the Colorado State Health Department sent a team to investigate. They submitted their report to our administration in the latter part of the month. Board members were given a copy of the report, and a copy went to the local newspaper as well. After the negative EMS report, I was sure Eve did not want to be secretive with a repetition of that situation.

The report listed more than a dozen rules violations. However, none endangered patient care. For one, the privacy of medical records had been poorly protected. Primarily, the new clinic had been lax in implementing and following the state rules since they had opened six months earlier. Eve followed up and corrected the violations, and this issue disappeared.

Then, late in the day on the Sunday after Christmas, I received a call from one of the EMT's. Their cell phones had gone out of service. The caller suspected that the phone service had been cancelled because of non-payment of their bill. I was appalled, again. This was critical for EMS because they were required to contact Mercy Hospital, 60 miles away in Durango, when they were transporting a patient via ambulance to the Mercy ER so that the ER personnel could prepare for their arrival. The cell phone was their only means of communication with Mercy while in transit via ambulance.

I told the EMT I would contact the cell phone company and get the service restarted. Unfortunately, Verizon wasn't open on Sunday evening. So, I called at 7 am the next morning, with more success. Indeed, the service had been stopped because the bill had not been paid in two months. I was able to pay the bill using my credit card. They said the service would be restarted within a few minutes. Five minutes later I called EMS and had them check their cell phones. We were back online.

You ask why I didn't call Eve or someone else in administration and have them handle the situation? First, I was the one called and so felt responsible for getting the service restarted as soon as possible. It was an emergency. Secondly, if I had transferred the responsibility, I had no assurance that there would be an immediate follow-through. I had lost confidence in our administration. This actually could have become a life-and-death situation.

I emailed Eve that same day and recounted the event and submitted a bill for reimbursement. I received a check shortly thereafter without any comment. This is a situation that should never have occurred. It further demonstrated that the administration was disorganized. I knew that bills were not being paid, but essential bills like this one, critical to the functioning of our service, had to come first and had to be paid.

Coming to the end of the year, I reflected on my nine months on the board. It had been a tumultuous time. Being the lone voice in the wilderness, so to speak, had not been an easy task. I explained the "affair" with Wally to some friends and citizens in the community and received strong support. No one believed I had actually assaulted Wally. Some even howled with laughter at the very idea. I did not doubt that my character would stand me in good stead with those who knew me. I regretted responding to Wally's taunting, but that was history now. Otherwise, I thought I had acted responsibly and couldn't think of any other action that I would have changed.

In pondering the Wally affair, I scoured my memory to see if I had ever been in a similar situation at any time before in my life. An eighth-grade episode popped into mind, the only remotely somewhat similar event I could recall.

We had been playing softball during lunch hour in the park next to our grammar school. I was the catcher. Someone hit a long foul ball. No one would go after the ball so I ran to get it. By the time I returned, they were about to start playing again with someone else catching. I yelled, "Wait a minute, I'm the catcher." My replacement said, "I'm catching now." I cannot remember the exact details, but we confronted each other. Suddenly, he hit me square in the forehead and knocked me down. I got up. I believe I inherently knew better than to hit him back. He was in a grade below me, but he was bigger and more muscular. So I grabbed him in a bear hug and squeezed as hard as I could in an act of desperation. I am sure I did not hurt him. I had no idea what to do thereafter. He did not react. I think I caught him off guard and for a few seconds he didn't know what to do. Fortunately for me, the school bell then rang, signifying the end of lunch hour. I let go. We looked at each other. I think we were both embarrassed. He turned away. My eighth-grade buddies started cheering and raised me to their shoulders and carried me back to the school building. I guess I was a hero to them, but I sure didn't feel like one. I recall just feeling relieved that the school bell had rung. That was the closest that I could recall to ever being in a situation similar to my present one.

By the time of the January board meeting, eight persons had applied for the two open positions on the board. Among the applicants were Dr. Jim Knoll; Dr. Bob Brown; Jim Carson, a civic leader; and Don Lundergan, my first board meeting friend. The other applicants I did not know, but these four were by now friends and, if elected, I knew we would be supportive of one another. I was also aware that Wally and Eve knew who my friends were, and these two undoubtedly would make an effort to see that none of them were chosen for the board. To thwart their effort I had recently re-read "Robert's Rules of Order"[14] and had come across an interesting legal ruling, "Cumulative Voting," which might help us. This said that, when more than one elective position was to be filled, a voter could vote for the same person more than once to fill the position. Before our vote, I explained this proposition to the Board. Betty said that she thought this was acceptable. I was sure she didn't understand the significance of taking this action. When we voted, on counting the votes, Betty noticed that both Ken and I had voted for Jim Knoll twice as allowed under cumulative voting. She threw out these votes with the support of Wally against our objections, with the end result being that a chiropractor and a woman I didn't know were elected to the board. Later, Wally queried our district's attorney about cumulative voting, and the attorney said that it would not be allowed under the Colorado Special District Association laws. I "Googled" cumulative voting and discovered that, whenever this provision had been brought up in court, up to the State Supreme Court level, it had been approved. I guess I could have gone to court over this matter but it hardly seemed worthwhile. However, I did get some perverse pleasure out of making the attempt to have the minority best the majority.

The other significant event at this meeting involved Eve hiring a bookkeeper in late December to bring our finances up to date. Perhaps our finances would now show some semblance of order and we would finally see the true situation?

Shortly thereafter Dick Babillis wrote a letter-to-the-editor in the *Pagosa Springs Sun* about a call he had received from this bookkeeper, wherein she recounted the woeful state of the district's finances: bank accounts had not been reconciled in the past year, payroll taxes (state and federal) had not been paid in six months, the district was swamped with delinquency notices, accounts receivable were grossly behind and accounts payable were just now being posted. Dick Babillis pointed out that the board chairman and the newly appointed treasurer, Laura, had said at the November board meeting that everything was "hunky-dory." They had only a couple things to verify before the financial information would be available. Dick Babillis in his letter asked, "What is the truth?"[15] It was clear where the truth lay. The bookkeeper's findings were consistent with what I had seen in the general ledger.

Jim Knoll, the chair of our Finance Committee in-waiting, and I had recently agreed that it would be useless to keep harping on the state of the district's finances. Since we didn't have the power to effect any change, it would be better to just let those in charge simmer in their own stew. The election was now just a few months away so our efforts should be channeled toward getting our slate elected. It looked like Eve, Wally and company were on a path of self-destruction anyway. They hardly needed any help from us. So, we didn't belabor the plight of the district's financial situation any longer.

In January, Kathy, our EMS ops manager, told me that a number of former as well as present EMT's had been under-paid, particularly for extra hours worked going back two years. She had submitted time schedule records to the head of the Federal Wage and Labor Bureau in Grand Junction but had not heard anything back. Kathy had had a hard time obtaining these records from Eve, and she wasn't sure whether these were accurate or complete. I said that I would check it out, and I called the Bureau. I had a good conversation with the person in charge. He indicated that he had met with Eve and that they had clarified the times and the monies owed. Some checks had already been sent out. He gave me the names of about six employees involved and the amounts they were paid. The others were in process and he felt that the matter would be completed shortly. He satisfied all my queries. I relayed this information to Kathy, which I believe resolved this problem. I don't know why this situation should have occurred in the first place, probably the result of sloppy record keeping.

This month I also ran into John Farnsworth, our former financial manager. He indicated that he was going to bring a lawsuit against the district via the Whistler Blower Act. He had brought a grievance against Eve for his improper discharge. Wally was supposed to have brought the grievance before the board, but he had not done so. Because John had been in an executive position, this was the proper procedure. He indicated that there was a three-month waiting period for discovery by both parties, so his lawsuit likely would not come up until after the election and a new board was in place. John indicated that he wasn't being vindictive, but he wanted legal redress and an apology to show that he had been wronged. I felt sympathy for John, and had I been in his shoes, I would have done the same. In the end, John won his lawsuit and got his apology and a settlement, both of which were well deserved.

The February board meeting was pretty much a replica of many of our past sessions: a war of words between the audience and Wally. I believe he enjoyed sparing with the crowd, and I believe he felt that he won most of these verbal exchanges. Had it been a debate, perhaps he would have scored higher than his opponents. Actually, Eve and company could not have picked a worse person to be chairman from their own standpoint. By his intimidation and quarrelsome nature, he angered the citizenry and turned them against himself, Eve and their cohorts. I doubt that Wally, Eve and their group realized that these words, as much as their actions, were doing them in. How in the world could they expect to win the election? In the end the citizens would have the last word.

The chiropractor who had won appointment to the board in January took the oath of office at that time and joined the board. The woman chosen for a board position was not present in January, but she did appear in February. She was pleasant and quiet during that session, which had its usual amount of acrimony. Afterwards, I introduced myself and said a few reassuring words to her. I noticed that Betty gave her a big hug and welcomed her, too. Significantly, she never appeared at another board meeting. I believe she was scared off by the anger expressed between the board and the audience. I couldn't blame her for dropping us.

CHAPTER 19

CAMPAIGN UNDERWAY

By early January, Jim and I had garnered through interviews and DQ lunches a complete slate of six candidates to run for the board election in May. We had two physicians, Jim Pruitt and me; a broker, Bob Scott; two businessmen, Neil Townsend and Bob Goodman; and a retired nurse, Pam Hopkins. These were all fine individuals, a diverse group who were well known as contributors to the well-being of our community. We felt we had a great slate that could run well against anyone.

Jim now formed a Political Action Committee (PAC) composed of the candidates and several people who were on our committees. Financial contributions were made by us and our friends to support the campaign. Our entire slate was running on the same platform, so one ad would carry all our names. Campaign buttons, posters, flyers and monthly newspaper ads were planned, and in the last two weeks of the

VOTE

for the candidates
your doctors stand behind.

Dr. Jim Pruitt - Neal Townsend - Pam Hopkins
Bob Scott MBA. - Dr. Richard Blide - Bob Goodman

When elected we promise
to heal the wounds of the past
bringing our physicians,
EMS, The Dr. Mary Fisher Clinic
and the community together again.

Be Patriotic to Your Country and County
Vote for Good Government

Check these candidates on the ballot.
MAIL BALLOT BY MAY 4

For all the details
www.prohealthcoalition.com

PROHEALTH

campaign we would have a barrage of radio ads. It was agreed that we would run a clean, informative campaign no matter what the other candidates might do. We were all eagerly looking forward to the election.

CHAPTER 20

A DOUBLE WHAMMY

Life sometimes has a way of tapping one on the shoulder and whispering in one's ear when least expected—sometimes for the good, sometimes not. The so-called "Double Whammy" had been nowhere in sight when we both got that shoulder tap that now precipitated my feeling melancholy and the urge to reminisce.

Following medical school in the 1950s and my subsequent post-graduate work, the first half of my professional life continued in academic medicine at the University of Maryland Medical Center in Baltimore, followed by a hospital-based practice as a pulmonologist and medical director at the Will Rogers Hospital in Saranac Lake, New York. Then came an unexpected divorce and a yearning for a change in scenery.

It was the mid-1970s when I sought that change in Dallas, Texas, where I was offered a partnership with Ken Cooper, M.D., at the Cooper Clinic and Aerobics Center. This offered a more upbeat type of practice, preventive medicine, than my specialty had been up to that time in chest disease. It offered the added benefit of allowing me to continue with my fitness endeavors, that had been up to then hiking and skiing in the Adirondack Mountains of upstate New York.

My new home was on some of the most beautiful grounds in central Dallas. Winding jogging paths amid landscaped greenery and spring-fed ponds interspersed with tennis courts and swimming pools and regal colonial-style buildings provided a relaxing environment in which to work and play.

Running would now become almost an obsession with me, all my new friends having the same interest. In fact, one of these new friends would become more than a running buddy.

I first saw her sitting by one of the swimming pools at the center wearing a bright yellow polka-dot bikini...just like the song. Discovering that she was single, I asked one of the clinic secretaries for an introduction. She did, with a twinkle in her eye.

Getting a date, however, was not so easy. My first request was met with a big smile and then, "Thanks, but . . ." followed by an explanation of having no extra time after her running, teaching, and caring for her son.

Not to be so easily daunted, I devised an invitation I felt she could hardly refuse. I knew that she was an avid runner. In fact, she had won the Dallas White Rock Marathon, women's division, two years before, and she had finished 19th in the Boston Marathon just the year before. So, I asked her if she would like a ride to the "carbo-loading supper" the night before this year's Dallas White Rock Marathon. After all these years, I still recall her words, "Well, I guess so. I don't have anyone else to go with." At least it was a start.

I was one of several runners planning to run the next day with Patti's best friend, Mary, to help her qualify for that year's Boston Marathon. That boosted my status several notches. Patti joined us for the last few miles of that run, which gave Patti and me a chance to get to know each other better. At the end I asked Patti for a date that evening. This time, she accepted without hesitation.

We went to Daddy's Money for dinner. While waiting for a table, we sat at the bar and shared a Margarita, each sipping on a straw from the same cocktail glass. Patti said much later, "I fell in love while looking into your kind, beautiful blue eyes."

The following spring I asked Patti to accompany me to ice climb on Mt. Rainier, where I would be the speaker at a seminar on mountain medicine. Patti had never skied or climbed in snow or ice before. We had a great time until a black cloud cast its shadow. While practicing an ice crevasse rescue, I was accidentally dropped fifty feet into a crevasse. Attached ropes saved my life, but during the free fall I struck an ice ledge and crushed my right knee. This necessitated our needing to get down the mountain to a hospital right away for treatment. A blizzard had developed, but my knee was obviously broken and now very swollen and painful, so we descended anyway. Patti showed her fortitude and athleticism by going down with us in a blizzard, at night in zero visibility, on a trail that was treacherous enough even when visibility was good. I was maneuvered down by sled handled by four climbers who had volunteered to join our group. We made it, getting lost once, but we had a remarkable guide, Marty Hoye, who a few years later lost her life on

Mt. Everest. We got to the hospital in Seattle, Washington, and I had surgery early the next morning.

I mention all this because it is part of a real love story. Patti, now Blide, is a remarkable person, not only beautiful and athletic but also charismatic and caring. We married within the year. Now, 32 years later, we look back at our many adventures as a blissful journey, more so than either one of us had thought possible.

All of this leads us now to how we handled the Double Whammy.

In early February, Patti and I decided we needed a break—not that we needed an excuse—so we joined friends to go snowshoeing on Lookout Mountain. It was a beautiful, sunny day, and we had fresh snow on which to trek. There were a dozen of us, mostly seniors like ourselves. This was a hardy, fit group that hiked, skied and snowshoed together all year around.

We were climbing from the base of the mountain to the top. It was fairly steep so we

On Lookout Mountain.

were snaking back and forth among the trees in a switchback fashion. I had trouble physically right from the start and fell behind. Patti stayed back with me as did Glenn Van Patter, our "tail gunner," assigned to keep track of any stragglers. I began thinking that I was really out of shape as I continued to falter and became very short of breath. We were moving slowly. I noticed that neither Patti nor Glenn was having any difficulty. We were so far behind that the others were now out of sight. I told Patti later that I knew I was in trouble when I saw that I could not even keep up with the "little old ladies." I meant this jokingly, with no disrespect to the women in the group who were all very hardy. It was just a shock to my ego-system.

I hated to admit it, but it finally imprinted on my brain that something was really wrong. I was huffing and puffing like I had never done before. I stopped and gasped, "I can't make it, something's wrong. I think I'd better go back down." No one disagreed. I'm sure Patti and Glenn saw that I was having real trouble. Patti suggested that Glenn go ahead, assuring him that we would be fine. Hesitating, Glenn responded, "I hope everything is all right." He turned and trekked upward, looking back frequently to make sure we were okay and on our way down. Patti accompanied me slowly downward, and we made it uneventfully.

On returning home, I called my pulmonologist, a chest doc, and made an appointment to see him. I had seen him previously for insomnia and been diagnosed with sleep apnea. He had placed me on a CPAP machine with oxygen to counteract the apnea and to help me sleep at night.

My present problem was obviously something quite different. While listening to my heart, my doc heard a loud murmur. He ordered some tests, including an echocardiogram (echo).

When I had the echo a few days later, I was able to lie on my side and watch the monitor as the technician ran the probe back and forth across my chest. I could see my heart and its contractions as the heart pumped out blood with each beat. Suddenly I saw what looked like a cord flopping freely in the breeze, so to speak. It whipped back and forth with each beat of the heart. I was fascinated, and at the same time I had a sinking feeling. I knew then that I had a serious problem for sure. I said to the technician, "That looks like a *chordea tendonae* (one of the tendons that connect the mitral valve to the heart muscle) floating in the breeze."

She nodded and said, "I think so."

The tendon had apparently broken free from the valve to which it had been attached.

Shortly thereafter my doc called to confirm what I had seen on the echo, and he referred me to a cardiologist, Dr. Bruce Andrea in Durango. I saw him the next day, and he took my history and examined me. He had reviewed the echo and said that I indeed, had a ruptured chordea tendonae. He also saw that the posterior leaflet of my mitral valve (one of two leaflets) was damaged. This was due to a Myxomatous degenerative process, thought to be genetic in origin. The echo also showed that I had severe mitral regurgitation to the extent that on contraction of the left ventricle half of the blood was pushed out of the heart normally into the aorta; the other half, however, was regurgitated backward into the left auricle (upper heart chamber) from whence it had come. The rupture of the *chordea tendonea* most likely had been the recent event that had suddenly exacerbated my condition and had made me so short of breath on our snowshoe excursion. The condition had been present and worsening for years, and as a result it had damaged the left ventricle (heart muscle) and enlarged the left ventricle and left auricle (lower and upper chambers of the heart). He said this was quite serious and could only get worse. The only satisfactory treatment was to have surgery to repair the valve. He recommended that I talk to a cardiac surgeon right away.

I had been noticing increasing shortness of breath on exertion for several years. In the past two years it had become more difficult to run, hike and ski. I recalled that two summers previously I had gone jogging with a long-time running buddy in Vail, Colorado. I had always been a pretty good runner, but now I couldn't keep up with him even though we were running slowly. I was really huffing and puffing. We even had to stop and walk on several occasions so I could recover. The next day he said he would not run with me because he had a race coming up and he needed to run faster to get in shape. In retrospect now, he probably was thinking that he didn't want to be there when I keeled over. However, at that time I just attributed my shortness of breath to getting older. At 72, I was five or six years older than he. Being a physician, you would have thought that I would be the first to recognize that I was ill, but when treating others, you can remain impersonal—your mind is not cluttered or confused by your own personal feelings. In my case, feelings of denial that anything could be wrong were paramount. Some individuals feel they are invincible until a catastrophic accident or illness shows them otherwise. Obviously I was one of these people.

In thinking back even further, I recalled that I had had an echo some 15 years before. I had a treadmill stress test as part of an annual physical exam and it had shown a transient arrhythmia (abnormal heart rhythm). I still had that medical record in my files, so I dug it out. I was aghast when I read that it showed "slight mitral regurgitation," the same abnormality that was causing my problem now. But the report stated that it was not hemodynamically significant. Even during exercise it was having no effect on the function of my heart. I vaguely remembered the report now, but I had forgotten all about this finding. I apparently had dismissed it as insignificant. My doc then had not mentioned that it was anything to worry about or that it should be followed-up.

Right after that medical workup I had run the Big Sur marathon in California. I had finished but had run some 30 minutes slower than my friends with whom I had trained. So, maybe it wasn't so hemodynamically insignificant after all. I thought no more about it back then. Patti and I had been competitive long-distance runners for over 15 years by this time. Even though we continued to run thereafter, our competitive racing days were over. Thereafter, I attributed my slowing down to age, which I am sure was partly true. Patti had "bad knees" so we, at least, were sure of the cause for her slowing down.

Undoubtedly, if I had paid attention to this problem and had it treated earlier, I would not now have been in so much trouble.

I talked to Patti about the findings and the proposed surgery. I was dubious about having major surgery in a hospital in a small town in Colorado. I was sure the surgeon would not be as experienced in open heart surgery, let alone the type of surgery of which I was in need, compared to one in a large metropolitan center. I knew several people who had gone down to Albuquerque, New Mexico, for coronary by-pass surgery and had obtained good results. I thought that would be my best option, but I needed to discuss this further with my cardiologist before making a final decision.

Now came the "double whammy." Several days later Patti came to me and said that she had just noted some vaginal bleeding. My heart sank. Both our first thoughts were that her uterine cancer had returned. I immediately called and made an appointment for her to see her gynecologist.

Two days later we saw Lee Ann Jordan, M.D., in Durango. I went in with Patti. On doing the vaginal examination, Lee Ann called me over to show me a small lesion mid-way up the vaginal wall. She biopsied it. This had not been there six months ago when Patti had her hysterectomy nor had it been there when she had a checkup just three months ago. It certainly looked like her cancer had recurred. We then had to wait several days for the pathology report to come back.

The path report came back positive for uterine cancer. I immediately called and made an appointment for Patti to see Dr. Bodurka, her gynecologist at M.D. Anderson Cancer Center in Houston, where she had her previous surgery. We felt very confident in her care, both as a surgeon as well as with her expertise in cancer.

We now had the dilemma of having two simultaneous crises, my need for cardiac surgery and Patti's need for further cancer treatment. Inasmuch as my heart condition had been coming on for awhile, I felt I could wait a little longer for surgery. We didn't know how much spread there might be in Patti's cancer so that needed to be treated as soon as possible.

It was at this same time that I had to appear in court regarding the October fiasco with Wally. The purpose was to set a trial date. My attorney explained to the judge about both our recently diagnosed medical problems and the need for immediate treatment. The judge was very compassionate. He asked if a date four months later, in early June, would be a satisfactory trial date. We happily agreed. I realized immediately that this would be after the election and would take the trial basically out as an election issue. I thanked God for this small blessing, a patch of blue in an otherwise dark sky.

We flew down to Houston and again checked into the Rotary House. The next day Patti saw her cancer gynecologist, Dr. Bodurka, who verified that the lesion certainly looked suspicious, and the path report left no question but that her cancer had recurred. The treatment of choice now would be radiation, so Dr. Bodurka referred Patti to a radiological oncologist.

We saw this specialist the same day. She outlined a five-week program of radiation, daily on weekdays for four weeks as an outpatient and then an intensive three to four days of continuous, localized radiation for which Patti would have to be hospitalized. She indicated that Patti would feel fine for the first couple weeks, but then she would develop nausea and diarrhea from the radiation. She encouraged Patti to drink lots of water and gave her a diet to follow.

When we saw Patti's gynecologist, we told her of my heart problem and the need for surgery, which we were putting off until after Patti's treatment. Dr. Bodurka smiled and said there was no need to wait; her husband was a cardiologist who worked next door at the Texas Heart Institute in St Luke's Hospital. She would speak to him to see if he could help us and she would give us a call back.

Dr. Bodurka called the next day and said her husband had made an appointment for me to see Dr. David Ott, a cardiac surgeon, one of the best in the country, with whom he worked.

I saw Dr. Ott a couple days later. His office asked that I have a tape of my echo "Fed-exed" down to him overnight. After examining me and checking my echo, he verified the diagnosis of Myxomatous degeneration of the mitral valve. He said my only options for improvement were to have either a repair of the mitral valve or replacement with an artificial valve. He said that he had done as many of these surgeries as anyone in the world. He could schedule the surgery for the day after tomorrow. I felt that he was squeezing me into his schedule and I had better grab the chance now, so I did.

Things were happening so fast that I had a hard time digesting what was going on. I talked to Patti after my meeting with Dr. Ott. We realized that, if I had the surgery right away, I would likely be sufficiently recuperated and out of the hospital before Patti became symptomatic from her radiation treatment. We decided to go ahead. It seemed fortuitous that events had worked out this way; my being able to have my surgery almost at the same time that Patti had her radiation. We would both be there to help each other.

As I mentioned previously, we were again staying at the Rotary House, which was attached by a bridge to the M.D. Anderson Cancer Center. One cannot give enough praise for the conveniences, amenities and especially the great care shown by the staff of this hotel to the hospital patients and their families. It was a Godsend. Patti said it was like being on vacation. She was always so positive, just one of her endearing qualities.

As noted earlier, when Patti had had her surgery for her uterine cancer, they had done a research study to outline the lymphatic drainage pathways from the uterus prior to removing the uterus. This was done by injecting a dye and a radioactive isotope into the uterus and then observing the flow outward into the lymphatic drainage system in the abdomen. We wondered whether this study could have caused the spread of her cancer. We asked Patti's physician, Dr. Bodurka, this question. She said this was not likely. Because the drainage would be upward toward the heart and not downward toward the vagina, I thought, too, that spread from this cause was unlikely. We were satisfied by Dr. Bodurka's reassurance. The spread of her cancer to the vagina must have occurred before she had her surgery, most likely at a microscopic level, so it wasn't observable until it had grown, which was some six months after the surgery.

My open heart surgery occurred two days later. I felt anxious but yet relieved that I was going to get this done. In mid-afternoon I awoke in the ICU. I was pretty groggy but vaguely remember Patti coming in, saying a few compassionate words and squeezing my hand. Dr. Ott came in, too, and said that the surgery had gone well. I was relieved. I remained in the ICU for two days and remember little other than the famous Dr. Denton Cooley coming around one morning on rounds. He stopped with his fellows at the foot of my bed while one of the docs briefly related my history to him. I tried to raise my arm in an effort to say hello, but by the time I was able to do so they were gone.

I remained in the hospital seven more days and gradually improved. I was able to go for a walk in the corridor daily, which gradually became easier. I recall Patti coming in on St. Patrick's Day and giving me a large, platter-size chocolate chip cookie covered with green frosting. She knew I loved chocolate chip cookies, but it made me nauseated to even look at it. I said nothing, just thanked her. I couldn't hurt her feelings. I never touched the cookie and it got dumped when I was discharged.

Patti visited me twice daily, the highlight of otherwise tedious days. It was just a short walk for Patti from the Rotary House, through M.D. Anderson Center and across the street. I was thankful that she was tolerating her radiation without any side effects yet.

One excruciatingly painful yet, in retrospect, somewhat humorous experience occurred during my recuperation. I had retained fluid on my right lung postoperatively so they were giving me an intravenous diuretic, Lasix, daily to make me urinate more, which would help get rid of the effusion. On my fourth post-op day, not long after the injection, I could feel the pressure building up in my bladder from the accumulation of urine. I tried to urinate but could not. I had been having symptoms from an enlarged prostate for several years. I was aware of men with this condition having to urinate but not being able to do so and having to be rushed to an emergency room because of the excruciating pain caused by the increasing pressure. Only catheterization, inserting a catheter into the bladder, would relieve the pain. Was this going to happen to me? I tried deep breathing and mental relaxation, thinking this might lessen the bladder sphincter spasm, but to no avail. I tried sitting on the toilet rather than using the urinal in bed—but again, no success. The pressure and pain increased relentlessly until it became unbearable. I rang for the nurse.

Joanne came in, and I quickly explained my dilemma. She immediately knew what to do and said that she would be right back with a catheter tray. Even with the terrible pain I felt embarrassed and thought perhaps I should have asked for a male nurse. That was just a fleeting thought. I needed relief and I needed it fast.

The nurse came back shortly and prepped me for inserting the catheter. Even though I was in agonizing pain, as she was holding my penis trying to insert the catheter, I noted a warm sensation and realized I might be starting to have an erection. I thought, "Oh God, don't I have enough trouble?"

I prayed that she would get the catheter in quickly. Then I could feel the pain begin to subside. The catheter had slid in. I raised my head and saw the golden urine running down the tubing attached to the catheter into the bag at the side of my bed. What a relief! Throughout, Joanne was very professional, kind and understanding. I could not have had a better nurse.

Patti came in that evening. I told her what had happened. She laughed, yet commiserated with me, too.

The next day Joanne came in with another shot of IV Lasix that had been ordered by my doc. I asked her if she thought this was wise. She said, "Doctor's orders," as I watched with trepidation while she injected the Lasix into my IV tubing.

Unbelievable as it sounds, the same thing happened as the day before. If anything, the pain was even more excruciating, just pure torture. Psychologically I knew what was coming, which I am sure increased my stress level and thus the bladder and sphincter spasm. Still, I went through the same routine as the day before; trying to relax, sitting on the toilet; all to no avail, again. I rang for the nurse. Joanne was on duty this day, too. We went through the same drill as the day before. No luck. This time she wasn't able to get the catheter in. This day there was no threat of an erection. She said that she would have to call in a urologist. I realized that this would take time, so I begged her to give me a shot of morphine to dull the pain. She did so. That took the edge off the pain, just making it a little less terrible. I gritted my teeth and tried to relax, knowing that I would have a long wait.

The urologist came about an hour later. It had been one of the worst hours of my life. Fortunately, he got the catheter in right away, and I again had that great sensation of relief, both mentally and physically, as the pain subsided.

The next morning I begged my cardiologist to stop the IV Lasix. He relented only a little and changed it from intravenous to intramuscular. That made me feel a little less fearful, but only a little. Fortunately, I had no further episodes of acute urinary retention.

On the ninth post-op day, I was discharged. I was still pretty weak, but I was happy to get out of the hospital and back to Patti and the Rotary House.

While at the Rotary House, we had internet access. Patti's brother, Michael, said he would communicate with both our families and friends if we would give him their email addresses. We emailed Michael daily about our progress, and he relayed this information to the others. In turn, we heard back by email from many family and friends regularly, which bolstered our spirits considerably.

By two weeks after surgery, I was doing well, though I was still quite weak. The weather outside was sunny and warm, so we took a walk in the small park associated with the Rotary House each day. The warmth of the afternoon sun felt great so we sun-bathed, clothed, each day, which was very soothing for both of us. The restaurant at the Rotary House was quite nice and had a good ambience, so each evening we enjoyed a pleasant cocktail and a nice dinner.

Into her third week of radiation Patti started developing diarrhea and nausea. Her appetite deteriorated and I had to encourage her to drink water and to eat. She finally finished her four weeks of radiation, but she was now in misery from the side effects of the radiation. She had medicines to blunt the side effects, but these helped only a little. By now she had lost quite a bit of weight, too.

A "ship's bell" had been placed at the radiation room's exit door. It had been donated by a former patient to serve as a means of letting the world know that a patient's radiation treatment was completed. After Patti's last treatment, she rang the bell three times, walked out of the room and smiled as everyone in the waiting room clapped, cheered and offered words of congratulations and encouragement. It was a tear-provoking ceremony, one that Patti and I remember fondly to this day.

As an aside, months later, Patti's brother, Peter, had a replica of this bell made. We placed it on a wall in our bedroom and we ring it now when we have something to celebrate.

Patti's outpatient radiation was finished, but now she had to be hospitalized for her localized radiation. They placed a specially-made cone in her vagina aimed at the lesion. This was strapped to her and then she was strapped down to the bed so that she could not move other than to elevate her bed by no more than 15 degrees. She could not get up, sit or even turn. She stayed this way for 54 hours while receiving the radiation treatment. I visited her daily and had to stand behind a lead shield, protecting me from the radiation. I could see that she was miserable and she said as much. It was hard for me to hold back the tears, I felt so sorry for her.

Finally, the worst of her ordeal was over and she was discharged in a much weakened state and still very symptomatic. We stayed several more days at the Rotary House until Patti felt she could travel. I gave her as much sympathy and support as I could.

We then flew to Albuquerque to stay with Patti's brother, Michael, and wife Helen for a day before we undertook our four-hour drive back to Pagosa. Being with Mike and Helen usually assured an evening of stories, puns and laughter. I believe they were both startled when we said, "Hi, which room?" and we struggled down the hall with our luggage and disappeared until the next morning. It was an exhausting trip for both of us.

On arriving back in Pagosa we first stopped to pick up our chocolate lab, Ghirardelli, who had been cared for by neighbors. She was one joyous dog, jumping and barking with glee. She immediately raised our spirits. No place had ever looked so good as when we pulled into the driveway of our home.

It took a couple more weeks before Patti really started to feel like her old self again. I was slowly recovering as well, gradually regaining my strength.

This had been a terrible ordeal for both of us. However, we realized that we had been fortunate, too. Everything had occurred like clock work, getting our appointments right away, having our treatments start soon thereafter; in particular, my being able to have my surgery right there while Patti had her treatment. We had received great care and fortunately had no serious complications. Patti remarked that her Blackledge (original family name) angel had been watching over us. I thought I was now ready to return and handle the health district's problems. This was a little overly optimistic on my part, as it turned out.

On a more humorous note, on our return I received an email from Norm

Vance. It contained a picture of Superman skiing, with my face supplanting that of Superman's. It said, "The Return of Super Doc." It was heart-warming. I framed it and still have it. Norm had made and circulated several cartoons in the past year mocking the board of directors and the administration of the health district. I appreciated his artistic efforts, as did many of the townspeople.

CHAPTER 21

BACK IN ACTION

As an aside, I ran a back rehabilitation clinic in Dallas, Texas, in the late eighties called "Back In Action."

A week after our return to Pagosa, all candidates for the health board election were to speak and answer questions at a meeting of the League of Women Voters (LWV). There were 12 candidates running for the six board positions, of which six were our carefully selected slate. Laura Mitchell and the chiropractor who had recently been appointed to the board were running as present board members. The other four candidates were new to the scene. Wally was not a candidate. I believe he was realistic enough to realize that he had little chance of being re-elected. He had virtually ostracized himself from the community by his surly behavior at the board meetings.

Our daughter, Leslie, was visiting so both she and Patti attended the meeting with me. The LWV had also scheduled the candidates for the Water District to speak, and they preceded us. Still recovering from my open heart surgery, I was now feeling pretty good in the mornings but by evening I would feel weak and tired. The hour wait for the water candidates to finish just aggravated my weariness.

The meeting was being held in the most spacious building in town, the Field House at the County Fairgrounds. We had an audience of four or five hundred people, a large crowd for a community our size, which packed the Field House. The twelve of us finally took our positions at the tables up on the stage. We each gave an opening statement. I paraphrased our "Position Statement" which was similar to what the rest of our slate did as well. This showed that we six candidates, who got to be known as the "six pack," were united in our vision for the future and emphasized that, if we all were elected, we would work well together. I didn't think that I did a great job, as by now I was feeling totally exhausted. Nonetheless, I thought the presentation was acceptable in view of my circumstance. Rather than looking at the audience, I concentrated on looking at Patti and Leslie which heartened me and gave me strength.

We then came to the question-and-answer portion of the program. The queries had been submitted by members of the audience and then screened by the LWV. All 12 candidates were to answer the same questions. The only question I can clearly recall was whether we should retain Eve Hegarty as our district manager. Laura supported her. Pam Hopkins, one of our slate, said she should be replaced. The other candidates, including four of our slate, said they would have to evaluate the situation before making a decision. That made sense for them and it was non-polarizing.

For my part, I stated that I had been intimately involved with Eve's work for the past year and so felt that I was in a position to evaluate her performance now. I mentioned that the mass clinic resignation was a catastrophe that could have been avoided. Then the opening of the new clinic using *locum* physicians, but not following the plan prescribed by Bob Bohlman and approved by the board, was unconscionable. Further, the district was now in a virtual fiscal crisis with a huge and still growing debt. Therefore, I continued, I found her performance to be unacceptable, and I would not retain her. I heard murmurs of agreement from the audience. There were a few inconsequential questions thereafter, and then the meeting was adjourned. I gave a great sigh of relief. I had made it to the finish.

As people rose to leave, I felt obliged to go out into the audience and say a few hellos. Both Patti and Leslie complimented me on my presentation, which buoyed me. I slept well that night, feeling that everything was now in place for the election.

One would have thought that the final board meeting before the election would have been quiet and sedate so as to not roil the waters before the citizens went to the polls to vote. Apparently that was asking too much.

For some time now, I had come to appreciate that we had exceptional reporters working for our local newspaper, the *Pagosa Springs Sun*. Tess Noel Baker and Tom Carosello not only accurately reported on the words and actions at the board meetings, but they captured the essence, the humor, the rudeness and especially the interaction between the crowd and the board. "Shakespeare wasn't this funny," "You're an Our Gang comedy," and "I'm not laughing at this; it's pathetic," were some of the comments at this meeting quoted in the local paper. There were heated shouting matches, finger pointing and nearly a chest-to-chest confrontation between two members of the public. The return to a "circus-like atmosphere" stemmed from a controversy surrounding the district's Drug Enforcement Agency (DEA) narcotics procedures as they applied to the EMS. Laura Mitchell accused our EMS ops manager, Kathy Conway, of giving false information to the newspaper. This was vociferously denied by Kathy, and so an imbroglio was precipitated. Wally finally said that this could be settled "lawyer to lawyer." The disagreement finally quieted down—only to be replaced by another volatile issue.[16]

The district administration had placed an ad in the newspaper: "We the professional employees of the Upper San Juan Health Service District support Eve Hegarty.... [We] are very fortunate to work with Eve Hegarty and are very happy to have her as our boss."

Joyce Little, one of these "professional employees," an EMT, retorted with a prepared statement. "How dare the administrative staff make such a blanket political assumption that I and all of my fellow professional coworkers support Eve Hegarty?" she demanded. "Was I asked if I supported Eve? No! Were any of the other EMT staff asked if they supported Eve Hegarty? No!" Little indicated that she was outraged by the statement, and other EMT's indicated that they were offended as well.

The administration's secretary then rose and took the blame, saying that she had placed the ad and that it had been "worded a little wrong," but not intentionally. My feeling was that the statement had not been written by the secretary but had to have come from higher up, and its intention was clear.[17]

Paid for by the district, this was obviously a political ad and thus unlawful, coming from a public agency. Blunder after blunder, this regime appeared to be fighting an inglorious battle right down to the end. As on so many previous occasions, I didn't know whether to laugh or cry. From a theatrical standpoint, I wondered if some of our citizens attended these meetings just for their entertainment value. They were never dull and, if you could remain aloof, they were certainly amusing.

BOOK II: A NEW DAY

Yesterday's preparation determines today's achievement.
                                                    - Anonymous

CHAPTER 1

THE ELECTION: A CLIMAX

The day of the election finally arrived. In the evening our candidates, friends and supporters met at a local restaurant, the Office Lounge, for cocktails, a buffet dinner, and to await the election results. The place was mobbed. The atmosphere was electric, alive and anticipatory but tinged with a little reserve as we all knew that nothing was certain until the "fat lady sings."

The polls closed at 7 pm, but it would take several hours for the ballots to be counted. Because there were two principal opposing factions, we had set up poll watchers throughout the day and had observers present during the counting of the ballots. We were taking no chance for any hanky-panky to occur.

Embers were glowing in the fireplace at the "Lounge," but the sun was still out and it was warm enough for the crowd to flow out onto the deck. There I bumped into Norm Vance. We reminisced back to 2002 when he began his first efforts to get a new board of directors. This had been a very stressful time for both of us, but more so for Norm because his wife, Ruth, had lost her job with the clinic resignation. As I mentioned previously, she had joined with Susan, the nurse practitioner, to open the Women's Clinic. We agreed that this showed that good people could rise above a disaster and come out on top. Jim and I had then been handed the baton by Norm, and we had brought it to this night.

After reminiscing with quite a few friends, Jim and I took a nostalgic trip back a year to when we had first begun this journey: the mass clinic resignation, the attempt to open a new private clinic, the EMS debacle. I left out my run-in with Wally, it not being something to remember. Jim's master plan had brought us to this point. Would we win tonight to culminate the efforts of so many people?

This was now two weeks after the LWV meeting, and I was feeling somewhat stronger physically. Still the recovery was taking longer than I had expected. Weakness and tiredness would still grip me late every afternoon to the extent that it was an effort to do anything other than rest in the evening. However, I had waited for this evening for over a year, and I would literally rather have died than not be here.

About 9 pm, while we were standing around talking and waiting in anticipation, the telephone rang. All went quiet. Then a big cheer began to roll across the room. Our entire slate had won in a landslide. We had all received four times as many votes as the nearest other candidate, with Dr. Jim Pruitt garnering the most votes. In my joy I admit to a fleeting thought of the other camp and what they must be feeling: utter despair and disappointment, I supposed.

The rest of the evening was one of joyous celebration, with a lot of back-slapping, toasting, and congratulations. I must have received an adrenalin rush or else my endorphins were maxing, or both, as I felt better and stronger and I was fortunately able to make merry with my friends. I thought about all the hardships I had endured in the past year and smiled to myself at the realization that it had all been worth the effort. At the same time I knew that the real, hard work of rebuilding the district was just about to begin. During the evening, Jim and I congratulated each other on a battle well fought. I again marveled at the "Plan" that he had developed and how we all had been able to carry it through to fruition without a flaw. This was really remarkable, when you stop and think about it. Of course, the opposition had helped by pretty much self-destructing. I wondered if they now or in the future would realize the error of their ways.

I ran into each member of our slate, and we congratulated each other. All were ecstatic and each mentioned that our real work was just now about to begin. We all looked forward to the challenge for which we had been preparing for some time now.

Patti, with tears in her eyes, gave me a big hug and congratulated me.

She had suffered along with me on many occasions during the past year. She agreed with me that the hard times in the past year had been worth all the effort. We looked forward to a better and happier year. I slept well this night.

COUNTERPOINT

I speculate that conversations like these occurred during this time:

A few days after the election Eve and Wally presumably met to make plans for the immediate future.

"Wally, I can't believe we lost, not like this, anyway. I expected some of their slate to win, but I thought that Laura and some on our side would win, too. We really got clobbered. I guess we were fooling ourselves when we thought the crowd was no more than Dick and Jim's cronies. What a disaster."

"A real bummer, Eve. What now?"

"I've been thinking. We need to save what we can. I will talk to my staff. I think we should all quit together as soon as I can clear my desk. I am not going to be a "patsy," coddle up to them and help in any transition. They never helped us; I'm not helping them. I think we should get together over dinner; the staff and us, and Betty and Laura too."

"You know my contract gives me six months' salary with health and pension benefits if I have to quit under duress, like harassment. So, I am quitting. I have been so heckled by Dick and his gang I do not think they can argue about the harassment. I want the whole check now; Laura can write it. I don't want to leave anything to chance.

"You know, Susan and Kathy have stuck by me through thick and thin. I want to give them bonuses."

"Eve, we can not give them bonuses without board approval. Are you thinking that we can write you a check without board approval, too?"

"I think we can, Wally. Let us have a dinner and then a board meeting afterwards. The meeting will be unofficial but we will record it so it will not look like we are doing anything on the sly."

A week later Eve, Wally, Betty and some of Eve's staff met at the Oakridge Motel.

"This is some spread, Eve."

"It's our last get-together, our 'Last Supper,' so enjoy."

After the dinner, Wally said they were going to have a board meeting. They had some last business to transect and Susan should keep minutes.

"We haven't posted this meeting and we don't have a quorum present. It won't be official, Wally."

"Do not worry, Susan. We are in charge until the new board meets. We don't have time to call an official meeting. This is sort of an emergency. If the full board were here, we would still have a majority so whatever we do would have passed anyway. Eve . . . ."

"Susan and Kathy, we are giving you both bonuses. You've stuck by me and you deserve them. I'm just sorry things did not turn out differently. Thank you for your loyalty. Wally . . . ."

"Betty, will you make a motion, first for Eve's bonus and then for those for Susan and Kathy?"

Betty made the motion and it was approved by Wally and Betty. Laura was not at this meeting.

As the meeting broke up Susan asked, "Wally, what should I do with the minutes from this meeting?"

"Put them in the computer with the other minutes. We need to make the meeting look as official as possible. The last thing we want is for it to appear that we took the money and ran."

Shortly thereafter, checks for Eve, Susan and Kathy were written and co-signed by the treasurer, Laura. This business was transacted without the knowledge or acceptance by the new board as well as before their first board meeting.

CHAPTER 2

TRANSITION

The meeting of the new board would not occur yet for two weeks. In the interim, Eve and her entire staff resigned. It would have been helpful if some of the old staff had stayed on for a short period to assure a smooth transition with the new staff. In any business, that is what one would normally expect. I am sure the old management team presumed that we would let them all go. I thought that at least one person, the secretary, Susan, who had always been cordial and helpful to me, might have stayed on. She had not participated in any of the partisan politics to my knowledge, except for selflessly taking the blame for the recent newspaper ad. But that wasn't to be.

Several of the new board members set up a meeting with Eve and Wally to make arrangements for the transfer of power. This turned out to be an acrimonious session, but both parties managed to get through it and accomplish what transition was possible. I stayed away, as everyone felt that I would just add to the bitter feelings. I agreed.

In the succeeding days we hired Dick Babillis, the former board chairman and a former district manager, to be our transitional district manager until we could hire a fulltime replacement. He was perfectly suited for the job, as his previous experience in these positions gave him a thorough knowledge of the district's inner workings. Though he had been a part of the previous board, he had quickly made it clear that he wanted to participate in our future. He had joined our finance committee in-waiting to help in the previous year.

Those board members who had met with Eve and Wally reported that the offices were a mess. We had heard that they had done a lot of paper shredding before they left. So Pam Hopkins, with some of the other new board members, spent a day cleaning up the offices. Dr. Jim Pruitt even took a day off from his medical practice to help. He said it was obvious that the offices hadn't been cleaned in some time. Jim Pruitt and I even talked about bringing in a shaman, an Indian medicine man, to do a dance to cleanse the area spiritually and bring it back into harmony with nature. However, we didn't follow through.

We then heard that some of the old board, namely Wally and Betty, had held an impromptu and irregular board meeting at a local motel with Eve and her staff. They had not followed the usual rules by posting the meeting to notify the public, nor had they informed the other board members of the meeting, which were requirements mandated by the Special District Laws established by the State of Colorado. The fact that they transacted district business made this an unlawful board meeting. Surprisingly, they kept minutes of the meeting. The secretary had typed the minutes and left them in the district's office computer. We found this document shortly after we took over.

The discovered minutes told of a dinner held before the meeting, seemingly a "Last Supper." What stood out like a sore thumb in the minutes of this quasi-board meeting was the disbursement of bonuses to Eve and two of her staff. Eve's bonus amounted to half a year's salary plus health and pension benefits. It was in her contract to receive these benefits under mitigating circumstances, such as harassment. However, to determine whether she met these contract criteria and the amount of money involved made it necessary for the new and official board to approve such a distribution of funds. The secretary and another fulltime staff person were both given healthy bonuses well in excess of $5,000 a piece. This figure was significant because the district manager was not allowed to disburse more than $5,000 on any one item without board approval. So, the entire meeting and the disbursement of funds was clearly unlawful. I suppose this was just another fitting ending to characterize that regime.

CHAPTER 3

NEW HORIZONS

Don't dwell on what went wrong. Instead, focus on what to do next. Spend your energies on moving forward toward finding the answer.
- Denis Waitley

A week before our first board meeting, our newly elected slate met at the county clerk's to take the oath of office. The initial meeting occurred in the third week of May. The first item of business was to elect new officers, especially a new board chairman. The only nomination to come forth from the board members was Pam Hopkins, a retired nurse. She was approved unanimously, including my vote. This event happened so quickly and without any discussion that it was clear that it had been fore-ordained by the other five persons on our slate. Of the six members of our slate that were elected, I was the only one with previous board experience. Her selection had never been mentioned to me. Were we going to repeat the error of the past board by choosing a chairman without prior board experience? However, I realized that the "affair" with Wally and the overhang of my trial yet to come would preclude my objecting. Though I felt assured that I would be found not guilty of the harassment/assault charges, there was no guarantee. If, by chance, I was found guilty, it would have been very embarrassing not only for me, but for the entire board as well. For this reason, although I had the experience, I would have been a poor and a risky choice for this position. Pam was certainly a good choice, and I heartily approved of her for the post.

I talked to Pam sometime afterwards and she indicated that the other board members had met and had discussed my taking the position of chairman. They felt that, in view of my recent health problems, it would be unfair to burden me with the tremendous workload that would now befall the new chairman. They were correct, and that made sense too.

I was asked to be board secretary, Bob Goodman would be treasurer, and Neil Townsend vice-chairman. We all accepted.

The next item on the agenda was a review of our financial situation. This was a cursory report, as we had no complete access to the financial records yet because there had been no sound transition from the previous administration. It was clear that we had been left with a debt well in access of $200,000. This was remarkable in that the last board had started the year 2003 with a surplus of $203,786, as reported by the auditor at the board meeting just a year ago. Plus, we didn't know how many bills were still out there and unpaid. As time would show, quite a few bills would continue to come out of the woodwork over the next few months.

I mentioned previously that we had established committees-in-waiting the summer before to educate the prospective board nominees and to help with the election. These committees were now formalized as statutory committees of the board. The members of these committees had attended the old board meetings and had stayed apprised of board actions, so they were able to help in the transition to the new era. To reiterate, these committees were Finance, Emergency Medical Services (EMS), Medical Advisory Committee (MAC), Citizen's Advisory, and Rules & By-laws. In addition, an ad-hoc committee was established to investigate the funds that had been recently and unlawfully disbursed by the previous administration.

A code of ethics had just been drawn up by our new Rules and By-laws Committee at our behest, and a motion was made to adopt this code. Its purpose was to prevent the types of transgressions that had occurred with previous boards. Too, it was to ensure that we would follow our own by-laws and the laws for special districts set up by the State of Colorado. This was unanimously approved. Toward the end of the meeting Jim Pruitt made a motion that Betty be asked to resign, as she had participated in the board meeting where district funds had been unlawfully disbursed without board approval. This act on her part violated our just-passed code of ethics. The motion carried by a vote of 6 to 1.

After the meeting, I was the first to congratulate Pam on being elected our new board chairwoman. This well-thought-of nurse and family person would show herself to be warm, personable and level-headed, excellent qualities that would stand her and us in good stead in the future. There was no ego problem with Pam that had to be fed by self-aggrandizement. She admitted that she had accepted the role with some trepidation, realizing that she was coming into a difficult situation with little experience. She now asked if I would help and support her in this new role. Of course I would. There was nothing more important to me now than to get things rolling in the right direction as soon as possible.

When Jim and I met after the meeting, we both expressed how grateful we were to see this first session get off to a good start. For me, it was the dawn of a new era after having been through a nightmarish year. Jim was now looking forward to getting our problems under control. And we did have major problems. We had inherited a huge debt and a failing clinic situation.

Each election year the Special District Association (SDA) of Colorado held a conference to educate new board members on the rules and laws of the SDA set down by the State. These associations, I believe, exist in all states in the Union. They exist to govern health, water, parks and recreation districts, etc. All of the new board members, including myself, attended this one-day meeting in Durango. We were all given manuals that included these rules and laws. Different speakers elaborated on specific parts of the manual. The "Open Records Act" was explained, whereby all public institutions were obliged to provide copies of any of their records to any of the public except for some confidential records, such as personnel records and minutes of Executive Sessions. Another was the "Sunshine Law," whereby no more than two board members could discuss district business outside an official board meeting. I had attended this same meeting the year before when I had first joined the board. It was very instructive for our new board members, and the repetition a year later was beneficial for me as well.

Another event now happened that was to benefit us down the road. One of our citizenry, Ron Clodfelter, had attended some of our old board meetings, and he had been literally horrified at how these sessions were conducted. Ron was a parliamentarian who worked with large corporations as well as with public organizations in helping them establish rules of conduct for their board of director meetings. He offered to sit in on our meetings and help us direct our meetings in a business-like manner. We now began using *Robert's Rules of Order*.[14] Ron sat next to our chairwoman, Pam, and offered his advice on any occasion when he deemed it necessary to lead her in the right direction. This was particularly useful when someone in the audience became unruly. This happened on occasion in our first few board sessions, but never again thereafter. A "You are out of order, Sir," pounding the gavel several times and then moving on seemed to work very well in quelling any untoward remarks. Ron was a big help in setting us on the right track, and we all appreciated his efforts in helping us.

Shortly after we began to rule, Pam consulted our district's attorney in Denver about both the unlawful board meeting and the disbursement of funds. He recommended that we have a special board meeting and go into executive session with him in attendance to discuss the matter. This would keep the matter private while we discussed the legal ramifications of these actions.

This meeting occurred shortly thereafter. Though I cannot release the details of this session, as their privacy is protected by law, suffice it to say that the board felt it was best to let the misdeeds of the past reside there and move on to the future. This session cleared our minds of some of the debris left over from the previous administration, and I know that we all felt better for having gone through this process with the guidance of legal counsel.

Finances dominated our June board meeting. Further bills had been discovered. Some had been discovered stashed away in drawers, and some were discovered only by the provider calling and reminding us that his bill had not been paid.

EMS was pretty much a constant, and expenses could not be cut. There was always a loss.

The same was true for the clinic, which was consistently a large "loser." The *locum* physicians' high salaries and the low patient volume kept expenses high and income low. This was a bad situation for which we had to find an answer. The obvious way to reverse this situation was to replace the *locum* physicians with new, permanent physicians who would practice in the community and who would be able to attract new patients. However, it would take time to recruit the physicians and then time for them to build up their practices. It would take one-to-two years after the new physicians were on board for our clinic to become financially viable. This offered a long-term solution but no help in the near-term.

A more immediate and practical solution appeared possible with the emergence of our new board. Could we merge Dr. Jim Pruitt's Family Medicine private practice into that of the district's public Dr. Mary Fisher Clinic? Now that Dr. Pruitt was on the board and his relationship with the other directors was good, this seemed like a feasible solution. When this was broached to Dr. Pruitt, he was agreeable to starting talks in this direction. The Finance Committee was delegated to begin negotiations with Dr. Jim.

The Finance Committee discovered that billing and collections were in a terrible state of disarray. Over $400,000 in uncollected patient bills remained on the books, many of them more than 90 days overdue. This was unbelievable, let alone unacceptable. The first order of business was to find a good billing/collection agency to help us handle this predicament. Outsourcing this debacle to an already-existing service appeared to be the quickest way to get this under control. Our interim district manager, Dick Babillis, was assigned to look for an appropriate firm.

Administration was one area where savings could be made. Eve had used two full-time staff in addition to herself (three when finance manager, John Farnsworth, was still there), plus several part-time staff members. To us it appeared that a full-time district manager should be able to do the job with one secretary. Dick Babillis had hired a new secretary, and they were already showing that this slimmed-down model was workable and efficient.

During this meeting, we weren't surprised to see Betty submit her resignation as a director. She read a statement wherein she lambasted the new directors for not supporting her, the previous board and their policies. In particular, she singled out the local physicians for not supporting the district. I believe that Dr. Pruitt's motion at the last board meeting, asking that she resign because she had broken our new ethics code, added to the bitterness of her remarks. This ended the last official vestige of rancor from the previous board.

An *ad hoc* committee had been set up to obtain and review applications for a permanent district manager and an EMS operations manager. The positions had been advertised, and a slew of applications had already been received. The contract for our present EMS manager, Kathy Conway, had expired but she was in the running for renewal of her contract. She was now on sick leave, having recently had surgery for back and neck problems which were believed to be, at least in part, work related. To fill the void in the interim, we were fortunate to have a couple, Brian and Joy Sinnott, who lived in town and had previously owned several private emergency medical services in California. They covered EMS part-time until Kathy returned, and their professionalism was greatly appreciated. The EMT's came to respect them greatly and subsequently wished that they would become permanent.

While still in the hospital in Houston, I had developed an arrhythmia (abnormal heart rhythm), atrial fibrillation, which decreased the function of my heart and also necessitated the need to take blood thinners to prevent blood clots. So, in early June I went into Mercy Hospital in Durango to be defibrillated, i.e., to have this converted to a normal sinus rhythm. This was accomplished, and fortunately the normal rhythm held. It made me feel significantly better. I eventually was able to stop the blood thinners, too.

By July the committee sifting through applications for district manager and EMS ops manager had chosen three persons for each position for the board to consider. A salary cap had been set for each position, commensurate with the limited funds available. As it turned out, the salary cap became a serious, limiting factor in obtaining good, experienced professionals.

We decided to have the candidates for district manager present their qualifications in person at the July board meeting. We were impressed by all three presentations. One of the candidates, Allan Hughes, was the consultant who had done the EMS report the year before. The most qualified by experience was a young man who had set up a critical access hospital in a town in New Mexico. The salary in his present position was higher than our cap, but he was included in case we felt we could raise the cap or he would come down. The third candidate was an older, retired person who had good prior managerial experience but he had been discharged from his last position.

The board discussed each candidate in public, going over each of their negative as well as positive attributes in front of them, which was admittedly embarrassing. We decided we could not raise the salary cap. That eliminated the top candidate, who indicated that he would not take a salary cut. It was agreed that the older applicant probably would not devote the time and energy necessary for this job. Though Allan's background was solely in EMS, he was finally chosen to be our new district manager. The directors would have preferred someone with a broader background, particularly in finance, but the salary cap prevented that possibility.

Two of the three candidates for the EMS ops manager position were not available for the board interview, so this was decided in absentia. Again, one excellent candidate was clearly above our salary cap. Another candidate had a questionable recommendation, and last minute checking showed he had difficulty getting along with fellow employees. Kathy Conway, our third candidate, had health problems. Would she be able to do the job? Joy Sinnott, our temporary EMS manager, made it clear that the position should be purely managerial; it should not require that the person be able to work in the field to make ambulance runs, lift patients, etc. Joy felt that Kathy's back problems should not preclude her from the position. Others questioned whether Kathy had demonstrated an ability to do the job in the past year. I supported her and pointed out that her previous tenure, working under Eve, had been very difficult and stressful. I didn't feel it represented the best that she could do. Some directors felt we should continue the search for this position. I persisted, saying I thought Kathy deserved the chance to prove herself based on the concerted effort she had made in the past year. In the end the board acquiesced, signing Kathy to a new contract as EMS ops manager.

CHAPTER 4

A TEST OF STAMINA

It was now some four months since my heart surgery, and I was feeling stronger, not at the level of the preceding summer but quite a bit better. I had been working out at our fitness center, rebuilding my strength by doing weight work and building my stamina by using the stationary bike and treadmill. Also, Patti and I had been out walking several miles each day with our chocolate lab, Ghirardelli. I decided it was time to give myself a real test and hike up Alberta Ridge on the Continental Divide, one of our favorite day trips. Patti was unable to go. She had been more aggressive than I in rehab and, as soon as she had recovered from her radiation and felt stronger, she had gone on several hikes with friends back in June and had aggravated an old back injury, leaving her now with persistent sciatica.

Ghirardelli accompanied me. We were going from 10,500 to almost 12,000 feet elevation so I knew I would be short of breath, but I hadn't thought I would be huffing and puffing like I was doing. Otherwise I felt okay, so I just maintained a slow pace. The trail switched back and forth up the mountain. It was beautiful, winding through the forest with the sunlight filtering through the conifers to dapple the floor below.

A ski lift for the Wolfcreek ski area sat at the transition from climbing to the ridge area. We stopped and rested and drank some water. GR was as frisky as ever and started chasing a squirrel down a rock slide. I yelled for her to come back. It amazed me to see her run so fast down rocks with no fear of mis-stepping or getting hurt.

We then had an easier trek along the ridge to a spot where Patti and I usually stopped for lunch. I had brought along my usual veggie sub, which I downed with water while GR lapped up her pouchful of water along with a handful of dog biscuits. I sat and enjoyed the panoramic mountain views, as far as the eye could see, with Treasure Mountain just across the valley, while listening for elk bugling in the distance.

After cleaning up, I bent over to tie my shoes. We then set out to retrace our steps back down the trail. I was feeling good. I had reached my goal even though it had been a hard, slow trek. I felt that I was on the come-back trail.

On arriving back home, I took off my sunglasses and reached for my regular glasses. No glasses! What an idiot! I instantly had a mental image of my bending over to retie my boots and my glasses falling out of my shirt pocket at our lunch spot. I even remembered mentally telling myself to pick up those glasses before I stood up. Alas, a brief moment later I had forgotten. I was given to self-admonition, but at least I knew where the glasses probably lay. Though exhausted, I vowed to repeat the trip the next day. I needed those specs. Would I be able to recover overnight sufficiently to repeat what was for me a rigorous hike? Was I pushing too hard?

The next day I was still pretty tired, but I was determined to retrieve my glasses while they probably still lay on the mountain and in one piece. My odd sense of humor pictured a near-sighted moose picking up my glasses and glorying in the vistas he could now see. I trudged up the mountain again with GR racing back and forth. Surprisingly, I did okay. It was just as hard as the day before, but no worse. And the good news: my glasses were right where they had fallen the day before. GR and I got to enjoy another beautiful hike and lunch. Two days in a row showed me that my recovery was coming along better than I had assumed. I was exhilarated. And some old moose out there was still near-sighted.

CHAPTER 5

ATTACKING PROBLEMS HEAD-ON

An *ad hoc* committee had been appointed the previous month to seek out new candidates to fill the board director position vacated by Betty. Jim Knoll headed the committee, which included me. We had come up with three good candidates but one stood out with a background that fitted our present needs, good grounding in finance and business and past employment in both government and private arenas. At the August board meeting Jerry Valade was presented as the nominee whom we recommended for this position, and he was approved unanimously. Jerry, a serious thinker who could be blunt in his criticism, also had a humorous side. I recall one situation where the finance committee had presented what seemed like an endless string of financial models for us to use to assess our monthly financial status. Jerry looked at the latest model and commented wryly, "I can make neither heads nor tails out of this report." Jerry became a good friend and valuable board member. Joining the board just four months after we had all taken office, Jerry was not that far removed from our new beginning. He had kept apprised of the district's past affairs and virtually had a running start when he sat down with us.

Our board knew it had an abundance of problems to solve and a lot of hard work to do. Now we were eager to put the "foot to the pedal." Finances took center-stage. The head of our finance committee and as sharp as they come, Dave Bohl, reported that it would be nip and tuck as to whether we would be able to meet our budget to the end of the year. Trying to catch up on overdue bills was taxing our coffers. He recommended that we request a line-of-credit from the Dr. Mary Fisher Foundation to cover any shortfall that might arise. A motion was made supporting this action to the tune of $50,000, which was approved unanimously. As members of the foundation board, Bob Goodman and I would make the request.

Next, Medicare had just notified us that we did not meet their requirements for reimbursement for ambulance calls taken to our public clinic or to the private Family Medicine Clinic. They stated that ambulance trips would only be covered to four sites: regular hospitals, Critical Care Hospitals, skilled nursing homes, and dialysis centers. They requested return of all payments they had paid us for this service. Why they were letting us know this now, after years of reimbursement, seemed odd; another government snafu just uncovered, I supposed. Fortunately, the amount of back payments they requested was not large, going back only a few months. It was nice to have a government agency being reasonable for once.

Just two months previously we had designated our Dr. Mary Fisher Clinic as the sole source for EMS to bring emergency patients locally. We had removed the Family Medicine Clinic as a designated destination to boost our income from this source. Now that we would receive no income from Medicare for ambulance trips to the clinic, we rescinded our previous order and allowed EMS to bring emergency patients to Family Medicine as well as to our clinic. Both clinics would still get the payments for patient care by their docs. This was the only fair thing to do for our local physicians.

Was there a solution to this new dilemma? Allan Hughes, our new district manager, had researched the problem and indicated that of the four designated sites, our only possible solution was to have a critical access hospital (CAH). He indicated that a CAH was a designation for small hospitals in rural areas. In the late '90s Congress had created this entity with financial incentives to help relieve the closing of rural hospitals due to fiscal woes. We designated Allan to investigate the possibility of our having a CAH and to report back to us.

It seemed like new problems kept cascading down upon us. The cost of an emergency ambulance trip from Pagosa to Mercy Hospital in Durango, some 60 miles away, was $2000. Some years before, the district had established an insurance policy for its citizens whereby for $25 a year, a person would be covered for one ambulance trip per year to Mercy Hospital in Durango. This was a popular form of insurance. However, the state now notified us that this could be construed as a form of uncertified insurance, thus illegal, and as such the district could be assessed penalties for continuing this practice. The board voted unanimously to discontinue this service by not soliciting new clients and to let lapse the presently insured. This decision was not popular in town, but the illegality of the insurance necessitated this action.

Interestingly, though we had only been in office a few months, the throngs that formerly attended these board meetings had dribbled down to just a few people. We looked on this as a sign that the townspeople had regained confidence in their health district board.

CHAPTER 6: TRIAL

GUILTY OR EXONERATED

By mid-August my trial in court finally came up on the docket, some 10 months after the fiasco with Wally had occurred. The date had been postponed from June because my attorney was involved in a murder trial that was extending beyond the previously-set court date.

It was a cool, sunny day, typical for Pagosa at this time of year. The court, contained in a new attractive town hall, was part of a community complex under development and was quite beautiful architecturally. This pleasant setting was accentuated by its site, resting on the banks of the churning San Juan River.

Patti and I met my attorney, David Greenberg, in the atrium of the building, where he took me through the events we could expect this day. As we began ascending the circular stairway to the courtroom, we could hear loud talking and laughter from above, rather unusual for a court, I thought. At the top of the stairs we saw Eve, Wally, Betty and Laura sitting in a reception area outside the court room, presumably waiting to be called as prosecution witnesses. Their conversation ceased when

The Pagosa Springs Town Hall and Courthouse.

they saw us. I said nothing but nodded to them, and Wally nodded back.

The courtroom, small but quite pleasant, had a paneled bar running across the front of the room, behind which were the judge's raised bench and several other desks for the court clerks. In front of the judge's bench were two long tables, one on the left for the defense where we sat; the other on the right for the prosecution where the district attorney would reside. Behind us was a bench that ran the length of the room against the back wall for court participants and spectators to sit. The décor was plain and a little bland, but this was a comfortable room and not at all cold or intimidating. Perhaps this just reflected my mood and feelings at this time, which were fairly upbeat. I knew I hadn't been as discreet as I should have been in the incident, but I wasn't worried as I had done nothing wrong. I had faith that the truth would reveal itself by the end of the trial.

The judge, appearing stately as he entered the chamber, walked across the room. We all arose. In his long, black robe and with his spectacles low on his nose, he appeared serious and judicial. I had a good feeling about him. He had graciously given Patti and me a long postponement of this trial because of our illnesses. As it turned out, I had needed all that time to recuperate.

The trial was to be solely before the judge. Initially, I had hired a general attorney in town to represent me. After taking me through the initial stages of the case, she recommended that I obtain a defense attorney and suggested David. I hadn't been aware of the fact that I had a choice of having a trial by a jury or solely by a judge. She hadn't told me of the choices, and the date for making this decision had passed, so it defaulted to a trial by judge. David made me aware of this situation. However, he indicated that this was a fair judge, and he felt this was the better choice. Not being comfortable with the whole affair, I was just as glad to have as few people involved as possible. I am sure I would have felt more uncomfortable being tried before twelve jurors who were my fellow townspeople.

Larry Holtus, the district attorney (DA) presenting the prosecution's case, seemed mild-mannered, not intimidating, and I had the feeling that he didn't have a great resolve in prosecuting this case. I wondered if this was sort of "fluff-work" to keep their seemingly quiet office busy. My attorney had indicated that in a larger venue, this case would have been too insignificant to prosecute. My brother-in-law, a justice in the Appellate Court in L.A., and his attorney wife both agreed that in California this case would likely never have made it to trial.

I was called as the first witness. The DA requested that I relate the events of the incident, which I did in a straightforward manner. He then asked some clarifying questions which weren't at all contentious. I did not get the impression that he was prosecuting this case with a whole lot of vigor, but then this was the first time I had ever been in a court room other than for about 15 minutes as a juror in the remote past. I think my comparison was to the many court proceedings I had seen acted out on TV, but these were usually about matters far more important than this trivial pursuit.

Wally was the next witness. Initially he seemed uncomfortable. He related his version of the affair similar to the interview report I had received from the detective. He did not mention that he had called me a foul name that instigated the affair and that he was virtually out of control after the board meeting when I was leaving the room. He said that I had called him an "a... hole" and had then hit him with the palm of my hand to his abdomen so hard that it ruptured his colostomy bag. He said this occurred while we were both on the same side of the table. I thought this was significant, because I had been sitting to the right of Wally. Presumably we would have been standing then and facing each other. If so, the others to Wally's left wouldn't have been able to see anything. Subsequently, he said, the contents of the bag had run down his leg, soiling his trousers and producing a foul stench.

I then walked around to the other side of the table, according to Wally. Next, I reached across the table and "tweaked" his nose while recanting my previous remark, saying that he couldn't be an a...hole because he didn't have one. I winced at the crudeness of my remark. Though I had heard and read this story a number of times by now, it still embarrassed me.

I wasn't quite sure what a "tweak" was, so I had checked my dictionary at home and found it to be a "twisting pinch." "Tweaked," "twisted" or plain ole "pinched," it didn't really matter. Wally had not been touched by me.

The DA queried Wally further regarding my words and supposed actions. He asked what had caused my outburst, and Wally said that he had done nothing to instigate the affair. I looked intently at Wally throughout his testimony. I wanted him to make eye contact with me, but he never did. I wondered if he believed his lies at some level, but I doubted that he could bring himself to lie right to my face. By now Wally appeared more comfortable. He even seemed to relish telling and embellishing his story to a captive audience.

Eve followed as the next witness. She seemed confident and unruffled from the outset. At times she could be so ingratiating that she made you feel like you were her best friend. On other occasions, such as when I went in to pick up the general ledger, she spewed hatred. I recalled that when I reviewed her personnel file sent to me by Texas Tech University where she had worked, they included a picture of her auto license with a photo from about 1990. The photo showed a lovely young woman in direct contrast with the hardened, overweight woman I now saw in the courtroom some fourteen years later.

Eve recited the story of the incident much as Wally had done, emphasizing the tweaking of the nose and the poke to the abdomen. When queried by the DA, she said she had noted a foul odor during the executive session. All of Wally's cohorts told essentially the same story. I wondered if Wally had rehearsed them. I didn't doubt that they had gotten together and discussed their testimony. Their descriptions of the attack all said I had "tweaked" and "poked." It seems that Wally was crafty enough to realize that, if they all told exactly the same story, it would appear contrived; hence, there were subtle differences in their recitations.

However, there was one significant difference in their stories. Wally had me on the same side of the table when I allegedly struck him in the abdomen, while the others had me on the other side of the table and reaching across to strike him. I thought that at least Wally realized that I wouldn't have been able to hit him in the abdomen from across this distance.

By now it was noon, so the judge recessed the proceedings for lunch.

David, Patti and I went over to JJ's restaurant, which was close by. We sat outside on the "beach," a beautiful setting on a deck down on the San Juan River which had been "re-channeled" a few years previously with cascading rapids constructed directly in front of the deck. Rafters and kayakers frequently "shot" the rapids directly in front of us as we ate. It was a relaxing, picturesque setting and a welcome reprieve from the morning's courtroom proceedings.

David went over the morning's events with us and appeared satisfied with how things were progressing. He had cross examined each of the witnesses. In particular, he questioned their recollection of the events that had occurred, but he didn't spend a lot time on this effort. I believe he felt there was no point in emphasizing something on which they were all in agreement. But he did his cross examination in such a manner as to make their statements appear questionable. He also queried their recollection of Wally's claim that his pants were soiled and that a foul odor was present during the executive session. I thought this was important because of the testimony yet to come.

I felt that David was doing an excellent job, and I had every confidence in him. To me this appeared to be a "walk in the park" for him. His demeanor in court exuded confidence which I thought was important for a winning attorney.

After lunch, the first prosecution witness was Betty. She appeared composed. She was holding her head high, perhaps suggesting some pugnaciousness. The first thing she mentioned was that she was a victim's advocate. I had

The view from the "beach" at JJ's.

the feeling that she looked on herself as having been a victim some time in the past. I wondered if she would change her mind about who was the victim in this case if I were found to be not guilty, a decision that would imply that Wally's charges were fabricated.

Betty told her rendition of the story similar to Eve's description. One thing that stood out was that each of the women was vitriolic in their description of me, which I supposed was an emotional reaction, whereas Wally's account was told in a more matter-of-fact, unemotional manner.

Laura was the last prosecution witnesses. She related much the same story as had Eve and Betty. When asked if there was any provocation for this affair, she mentioned their shock at the final EMS report that I had revealed at the board meeting. I thought it significant that she said that "they" were all aware of the EMS report and considered it a "non-issue." Recall that I had the feeling, when I revealed the final EMS report back in October, that other board members were already aware of the report. Laura apparently did not feel that the rest of the board members, namely Ken and me, and the public had a right to see the report as they kept their knowledge of the report secret, too.

David's cross examination of both Betty and Laura was brief and straightforward, again not dwelling on the details.

This completed the prosecution's case against me. It was now 4 pm, some 7 hours after we had begun. I, for one, was tired. I have to say that I actually found the trial very interesting while sitting and observing the course of events. It was somewhat like watching Court TV, a surreal, out-of-body experience, watching this character who was being accused of harassment and assault. I think that my experience as a physician had made me somewhat immune to all these false accusations. The stress and strain from practicing medicine for 44 years had imbued me with a thick skin.

All of the DA's witnesses had to remain waiting outside the courtroom until the proceedings were completed, so I assumed they were tired, too. For them, sitting outside had to have been a pretty boring, tedious day.

David requested a brief recess, which was granted by the judge. He wanted to apprise me of how he was going to proceed with the defense. He would be calling just two witnesses, Ken Morrison and Kathy Conway. He didn't feel a need to put me on the stand, but he would do so if I insisted. Personally, I had a strong desire to counter many of the statements that had been recited by the prosecution's witnesses and to tell my side of the story. David did not feel that this would accomplish anything positive. He thought that the judge would see the conflict in their stories, which would be better than anything that I could add. I deferred to his judgment.

David's first witness was Ken, my fellow board member, with whom I usually agreed on policy. I had talked to Ken some time before and then realized that he hadn't been present in the conference room when the incident with Wally had taken place. He related that he had gone to the restroom as the audience was breaking up after the board meeting and had returned just before the executive session started. He had missed the whole encounter. If he had been present, I am sure that this trial would never have occurred. As it was, only the "Gang of Four" was present, which gave them the opportunity to give testimony without contradiction except for mine.

Ken was out of town and not able to appear in court so he testified via speaker-phone. David brought out two important points. First, Ken had gone to the restroom just before the incident and had returned just before the executive session started, which covered the entire time between the two sessions. Ken neither saw Wally in the restroom nor did he pass him in the hall. Eve had said that Wally told her that his seal was broken and that he carried extra seals with him, intimating that he had gone to the restroom to change the seal. The second point was that Ken had not noticed any soiling on Wally's trousers and he hadn't noticed any foul odor during the executive session. The stench from such an occurrence would have been noticeable to all, not just to the three who were now supporting Wally's claim.

The DA did not cross-examine Ken. He had done an honest and accurate recounting of his recollection of the affair, to my way of thinking. I was thankful for his testimony supporting the truth of the affair.

The last witness was Kathy Conway, our EMS ops manager . The DA had talked to her previously and was familiar with the testimony she was about to give. As well, the detective who had done our original interviews had queried her later, and I had received a copy of this interview.

In the preceding months Kathy had undergone three surgeries, a fusion of her lumbar spine and then a fusion of her cervical spine. When they operated on her neck, they had discovered that she had thyroid cancer, which necessitated a third surgery. This was then followed by radiation to this area. So, she had been through an unbelievable, prolonged ordeal. I knew that this had been both physically and mentally exhausting for her. Having completed her physical therapy, she was now in rehabilitation. I was honored by her appearance to testify while in obvious discomfort and pain.

Kathy came into the courtroom on crutches. I could see that she was laboring and uncomfortable. I felt guilty that she had come, but she had insisted that she wanted to testify. She took the witness chair and swore to tell the truth. Then David asked that she tell her story.

Kathy stated that Wally had come into her office at work a week or so after the incident. He had closed the door, sat down, and told her his version of the incident. After the board meeting had ended, he told her that he was purposefully making inflammatory remarks, trying to goad me into retaliating against him. However, he didn't tell her that he had called me a "f...bastard." He then related the rest of the story similar to what he had told everyone later.

At the time Kathy had no idea why Wally was telling her this story. She thought that perhaps he was trying to curry her favor. He knew that Kathy and I were like-minded acquaintances and that I had staunchly supported her on many occasions. I supposed that by telling her this tale, Wally felt that he was demonstrating his power while at the same time tearing me down. I thought it showed desperation on his part, trying in such a sophomoric way to enhance his own image.

The DA made no effort to refute Kathy's testimony. Afterwards, she rose slowly from her chair, obviously in discomfort. She asked for help in picking up her purse from the floor, being unable to bend to retrieve it. She then exited slowly on her crutches. This had to be quite an ordeal for her, to come forth while having so much pain and do what she thought was right. I greatly appreciated her effort.

The DA and David then made their closing statements, both of which were brief. The prosecutor put emphasis on my words and the supposed assault, while David emphasized the contradictory testimony.

The judge said that he would render his decision in several weeks and that we would receive his decision by mail. He then adjourned the session.

Afterwards, David said that he thought that the trial had gone well, and he wasn't worried about the decision. I thought so, too, but I was glad to hear him verify my impression. On parting, he said he would call me when he received the rendering to answer any questions that might have arisen in my mind from the report.

Patti and I went out for dinner that night to recount the day's events and to relax. Throughout the day, Patti had been like the Rock of Gibraltar, sitting next to me and supporting me with her comments. We both felt the trial had gone well. I thought it likely that the judge would find in my favor. In any case, this was a pretty minor affair, and my attorney had indicated that the worst that could happen would be that I would receive a fine. Though this whole episode had been an unfortunate affair, I was happy that the "Gang of Four's" plan had been foiled by timing, for it had no effect on the election. If anything, it had backfired on them and had garnered support for me.

Several weeks later I received the judge's decision in the mail. He found me guilty of harassment because I had called Wally an a...hole. I asked my attorney why the judge had not taken into account Wally first calling me a f...bastard. He said I had not brought harassment charges against Wally, so this would not matter and would not nullify my comment.

On the charge of assaulting Wally, I was found not guilty, the judge indicating that there was insufficient evidence to support the charge. I thought it likely that the judge saw through the prevarication of Wally and his supporting witnesses. I had clearly realized that the strength in the prosecution's case was the agreement by all four that I had physically touched Wally. I felt that the testimony of Ken, and particularly that of Kathy, had helped in my defense.

I ended up paying a fine of $100, which broke down to $75 for the harassment charge and a $25 court fee.

I was satisfied. I felt that my attorney had given me an excellent defense. I couldn't have asked for anything better. I did wonder what Wally and his cohorts thought about the whole affair now. I suppose they obtained some satisfaction from putting me through this grueling process. For my part, I thought that it just put another topping on all the thoughtless and sordid events that they had put the community and me through in the past year.

CHAPTER 7

CRITICAL ACCESS HOSPITAL

Our district manager, Allan Hughes, was right on the ball and had contacted the head of the Colorado critical access hospital organization in Denver, Lou Ann Wilroy. He arranged to have her make a presentation on critical access hospitals to the directors at a special board meeting.

As Lou Ann, an attractive, slim brunette, began her presentation, I was impressed by her polish and professionalism. She started with facts that led up to new, major health care legislation being passed by Congress in 1997. Rural areas for many years had fallen behind urban areas in quality of health care for several reasons. Family physicians are the primary health care givers in small towns across America. Of all the medical specialties, family medicine receives the lowest reimbursement for patient care by both private and federal insurance programs, making this a lower-income type of practice. Rural physicians do not have immediate access to specialists or access to modern, up-to-date medical equipment and facilities as do their urban brethren. So, fewer physicians are attracted to this type of practice. The increasing dearth of this type of provider had resulted in longer work hours for those practicing in the country, which made this kind of practice even less appealing. To make matters worse, hospitals in rural areas were among the worst hit by the ever-decreasing reimbursement by federal and private insurance in the government's attempt to rein in the burgeoning cost of health care in the country. Many of these hospitals were forced to close for financial reasons.

This all came to a head in the mid 1990s as a crisis in rural health care was looming. Congress paid attention. In 1997 it passed the Balanced Budget Act that aided rural health in two ways. The first enhancement was to promote the establishment of hospitals in rural areas to be called critical access hospitals (CAH's). To make this financially viable the law provided that reimbursement for hospitalized Medicare patients would be at 101 percent of cost, far better than what existed for urban hospitals.

The second enhancement was the establishment of rural health clinics where Medicare would reimburse patient fees almost 50 percent higher than for like patients in urban areas. The half dozen plus years that have passed since enactment of this law has shown this to have probably been the most effective rural health care legislation to have been passed in the last half century or more. It was a life saver literally for rural hospitals and for docs practicing in rural areas, not bringing them to the level of their urban brethren but making survival possible and more manageable.

The board was very attentive to Lou Ann's exhortations, as was the audience in attendance. She continued, relating that there were presently 25 CAH's in Colorado. One significant difference between the existing CAH's and our situation was that they all had pre-existing hospitals, and with the passage of the new law they either had updated their existing hospitals or had built new hospitals. We would be the first completely new CAH without a preceding hospital if we chose to pursue this course. However, she didn't see that this posed any problem from a regulatory standpoint. She then easily fielded questions from the board and audience. There didn't appear to be any major stumbling block to our considering building our own CAH. I, for one, was enthused by her presentation.

Afterwards, the board discussed the pros and cons of taking this large step forward in our community. The closest hospital to us was Mercy Hospital in Durango, some sixty miles and an hour's drive away. In the winter, snow conditions could make this a longer and a much more hazardous trip. So, there was no denying that a facility in town to provide at least semi-critical medical care would be a big asset.

Some questioned the financial feasibility of such an endeavor, particularly for a small community. Also, would there be a sufficient patient load and would our local doctors be willing to add this additional responsibility and work to their already busy outpatient clinic practices?

These were all questions for which we had no ready answers. So, at this point no one was gung ho on going ahead with such a project, but everyone was interested in obtaining more information.

On talking to Lou Ann after the meeting, she mentioned that we could apply for a state grant to provide funds to hire a consultant to study the feasibility of building a CAH in our community. At this time the district did have a grants committee, Tom Steen, as the head, and me. At our next board meeting we sought permission to apply for this grant, and this was unanimously approved. It was a no-brainer. We had everything to gain and nothing to lose.

In preparing the grant, Tom and I had to gather quite a bit of data to fill out the application. We found that of the 25 CAH's in the State of Colorado more than half were in population areas smaller than our health service district. By far the majority of these hospitals met their budgets and were at least marginally profitable. No one expected a large profit inasmuch as Medicare reimbursement was no more than 101 percent of cost. The goal was to break even. We submitted the grant soon thereafter.

Following the meeting with Lou Ann, I had talked to Dr. Jim Pruitt, and he mentioned that the town of Del Norte, some 60 miles to our east, had the previous month just opened a CAH. Pruitt had attended their open house and was quite impressed with their new facility. He gave me the name of their medical director, Dr. Norman Haug, who had been the instigator and leader of the project over its four years in development.

Being very enthusiastic about the idea of a CAH, I called and made an appointment to meet with Dr. Haug. Patti came with me. Norman is a large man, the archetypical country physician. He seemed a little reserved initially but, as he showed us around and told us of his problems and solutions, we warmed to each other. It was clear that he had taken on a huge endeavor, had toiled for years, and now was very proud of what he had achieved—as he should be. I explained our interest in visiting him and seeing his facility inasmuch as we were considering building a CAH ourselves in Pagosa Springs. He was very interested in our endeavor and said he would be glad to help us in any way he could.

Norman started by showing us their beautiful lobby and reception area, which had a small cafeteria nestled to one side. Next he showed us a wing of 11 beds with room for expansion. Half the beds were presently occupied, which I thought was excellent for having been open just a few months.
The emergency area was immediately adjacent to this wing and had been built so that the two areas could share staff, a smart decision for greater efficiency in using personnel. They had a large laboratory area, necessary for all the outside laboratory work they did for other facilities, including Dr. Pruitt's Family Medicine Clinic in Pagosa.

They had a roomy radiology area for which they had purchased a new CT scanner. The family practitioners read some of their own CT scans, but for the most part they telemetered the scans over to the larger hospital in Alamosa, another 50 miles to their east, for expert opinions from their in-house radiologists. This was a 24/7 operation and a neat, modern setup. This allowed a rural hospital and physicians to access the same expert radiology service available in large urban areas.

They even had a small surgical suite with one operating room and a room for minor surgical procedures, plus an adjacent recovery room. There was even an area for specialty services wherein specialists from out of town could come in and see patients. They had a small pharmacy and an area for physical therapy. In essence, this was a larger hospital in miniature. I was very impressed, to say the least. I wished that some of our other board members had accompanied me to see what a community similar to ours had accomplished.

Afterwards, Norm filled us in on some of the important features and problems he had encountered over the four years of the project. The total cost of the hospital had been $12 million, of which $10 million was raised by a local bond issue. They raised one million from private donations. Another million came from grants, including $500,000 from a Colorado State Mineral and Energy grant. They had not always picked the right firm for different portions of the project, which had necessitated a change in management in mid-stream on some occasions.

As opposed to our possible project, Del Norte had an older existing hospital dating back to the early '50s, so the local physicians were proficient in both inpatient and outpatient practices. I had no doubt that our local docs would adapt to both types of practice, also.

I was greatly impressed by what Dr. Haug had accomplished, and I told him so. I told him about our thoughts of converting our clinic, the Dr. Mary Fisher Medical Center, into a critical access hospital. He thought this would be a wise decision and again very generously offered to help us in any way he could.

The trip to see the new Del Norte CAH was quite inspirational for me and encouraged me to increase my efforts for our own CAH. Patti was just as enthusiastic and supported my efforts in this direction. Afterwards, I wrote up a report of our visit with Dr. Haug and gave a copy to each of our board directors and to our committee members.

CHAPTER 8

PLANNING COMMITTEE

At our September board meeting the finance committee reported that they had failed in their talks with Dr. Jim Pruitt and Family Medicine to come up with a plan to merge their private clinic with our public clinic. They had come close to an agreement, but in the end they couldn't reach a satisfactory financial arrangement. I did wonder if there wasn't more to this failure than just the financial disagreement. From the meetings Jim Knoll and I had with Jim Pruitt, it was obvious that he was uncomfortable about making any formal arrangement with the district. He had watched the ups and downs of the district for some 20 years. The recent experience of the Dr. Mary Fisher Clinic staff resigning en toto just the year before would have reinforced his feeling of the need to stay at arms'-length from the district. After all, he had two of our former clinic staff on his team now to warn him about forming any such alliance. Too, his partner, John Picarro, hadn't appeared particularly interested in this joint enterprise. Jim mentioned on one occasion, "What happens in the future when another board is in place with new directors?" The implication was that new directors might not be as friendly as the present ones. Of course, no one could guarantee him a favorable future.

Following the finance committee's report on this failure, I thought perhaps a physician being involved in the talks on our side would have been of benefit. After all, the negotiations had been physicians vs. businessmen, and I wasn't sure our side had looked at the merger from a physician's standpoint. I suggested that a new *ad hoc* committee be formed to include a physician as well as the finance committee members. This suggestion fell on favorable ears, and the board passed a motion creating this *ad hoc* planning committee. Jerry Valade, new board member, would head the committee, and I would be an advisor to the committee. Only two board members could be on a committee because of the state mandated "Sunshine Law," in this case Jim Pruitt and Jerry Valade. Dave Bohl and J.R. Ford from Finance, who had sat on the prior committee, would sit on the new committee as well. Was it presumptuous on my part to think that we could improve on the finance committee's efforts? Perhaps! I just hated to give up on this effort, which I felt would be positive for both parties. Jim Knoll, too, was a strong proponent for this merger.

Shortly thereafter Jerry came down with pneumonia, so I was designated to take over as chair of the committee temporarily. We began meeting immediately and met subsequently every two weeks. The finance committee had already developed a cursory district budget for the coming year, 2005, which formed the basis for the financial models that we presented to Dr. Pruitt. It would have helped if we had had financial data from Family Medicine to integrate into our models. However, Jim Pruitt would not release any information about their group's finances. However, I had a pretty good idea what their income and expenses were so I used these figures in the subsequent models we presented to them. I had gleaned this data from bits and scraps of information that they had dropped from time to time in our various meetings. The budget and the models also contained the tax monies delegated to the clinic.

There were four areas in which Family Medicine would benefit financially by associating with the district. First, they would be paid by us for providing 24/7 after-hours and weekend coverage, which was in addition to the patient fees they billed during these hours. Second, in their present system the fees they received for seeing Medicaid patients were so low that they did not meet their expenses. Then there were patients who could not pay at all or who paid on a sliding fee scale proportional to their income. They lost money in all these areas as well. Many medical practices did not accept Medicaid patients or those who couldn't pay. However, Dr. Pruitt never turned away a patient because they couldn't pay, and this was not an insignificant part of their practice. Still, they managed to survive. We proposed to make up the difference between what they received from these three losing areas to what they would receive if these patients were on profitable, private insurance. Both of these provisions gave them income above and beyond what they were making now and with no extra work or time involved on their part.

Third: from the Balanced Budget act of 1997 we proposed to become a federally designated rural health clinic, thereby qualifying for higher fees on Medicare patients. Too, there was a state designation for a public clinic to receive higher fees on Medicaid patients. So, there were multiple ways in which we could quite significantly increase the income for the physicians associating with us.

Fourth, they would move into the Dr. Mary Fisher Clinic building, which was larger and a more modern facility than their present building and we would charge them only a nominal lease fee.

Jim owned his clinic building, on which he still had a mortgage. He expensed this out in their practice by dividing the mortgage payments among the practicing staff as a monthly cost of doing business. On one occasion Jim mentioned that his building was his pension. On retirement he would sell the building to his partners and use the funds for his retirement. So it was obvious that our plan would jeopardize his retirement plan. J.R. Ford proposed taking on the task of leasing out the space in Jim's building after their staff had moved into the Dr. Mary Fisher building. His feeling was that it would be easy to lease this space to businesses in town that would benefit from a close association with this developing medical complex. This made sense, and actually Jim should come out ahead as it was likely that there would be an increased income with a decreased expense. Of course, there would be the expense of renovating the building to accommodate the new tenants. I should mention here that there were three buildings in close proximity that made up this budding medical complex, including the Dr. Mary Fisher Medical Center (clinic) and a building owned by J.R. Ford that contained a small medical laboratory and a physical therapy practice. The latter building was on district property and leased to J.R. on a long-term basis. The third building was Family Medicine, owned by Dr. Jim Pruitt, which was on private land immediately adjacent to the Dr. Mary Fisher Clinic.

For the most part, our meetings were just with Jim and did not include his partners, though he kept them apprised of our negotiations. We usually met from 7-to-8 am in Jim's conference room, before he started seeing patients. On occasion we met at The Elkhorn Cafe in town for an early breakfast meeting. Their breakfast burritos are to die for.

The first obstacle we encountered was that Jim and his group had decided that they did not want to move into our clinic building, preferring to stay in their own facility. It was apparent that their thinking was two-fold. First, they didn't want to take the financial risk of leaving their building. Secondly, they probably still didn't trust the district long-term. If they had a disagreement with the district in the future and they had to return to their building, they would first have to evict the tenants and then renovate the building to meet their needs, probably a year-long project. However, I think the main objection, again, was one of long-term trust. It was a risk vs. reward issue. Why should they jeopardize their present fairly comfortable status for the reward of making more money? I could see their position, and I'm not sure but what I wouldn't have thought likewise had I been in their shoes.

We continued the talks but left out the idea of their moving into our building, for this was not a necessity and wouldn't squelch the negotiations. We tweaked a variety of budget models to suit Jim's requests. Then a major problem arose. They asked that we guarantee a substantial sum of money as part of the contract. We evaluated this request and came to the realization that we could guarantee that portion that we were sure to receive from tax monies. Being a public, government entity, it would be illegal to enter into a contract guaranteeing more than this amount. This did not sit well with them. From our side, I thought their request was unreasonable. Adding the income from patient practice fees to the tax monies expected more than met their requirement, but legally we could not guarantee this amount. They stuck to this guarantee as part of any agreement.

Finally, by mid-December, it became apparent that we were not making any progress. So, at this time we halted the negotiations. We had failed, as had the finance committee the summer before and, to boot, we had wasted another three months in trying to resolve our clinic problem.

Again, as mentioned previously, I believe it wasn't the finances that did us in, but the matter of long-term trust. I believe the "guarantee" request was their polite way of ending the negotiations. They had not turned us down, but rather we weren't able to meet their demands even if it was an unreasonable request. Jim Pruitt had always been fiercely independent, and he wasn't going to change. Perhaps we should have brought up the matter of trust at the beginning of negotiations before we began any financial palaver. In retrospect this would have been the smart thing to do and might have saved a lot of time. On the other hand, I'm not sure Jim would have admitted to not trusting us, or those who would follow us in the future. I believe he might have thought that such an admission would have diminished his stature in the eyes of his fellow board members and impaired his performance on the board in the future.

So, now we were in the same situation as six months previously. We still had a clinic with too little income and too high expenses. The *locum* physicians had been unable to build up their patient base. What patients we had were primarily tourists and transients. The local citizens wanted a physician with whom they could develop a long-term relationship, so they went to Dr. Pruitt's Family Medicine, as did Patti and I and the other board members. This may have seemed hypocritical on our part, giving verbal support to our public clinic while actually using the private docs for ourselves and families. But this clearly exemplified the problem with our clinic. Why would you expect anyone to leave their long-term physician for one who was going to be here only temporarily? Not until we could get physicians who would practice in our clinic permanently would we be able to build up the patient load at the clinic. This was the fatal flaw in establishing the new clinic in the first place. You cannot build a practice using temporary physicians unless the citizens have no other choice. You can start a clinic this way but you will have to recruit physicians who want to practice there permanently to build a viable practice. We had not been able to accomplish that goal.

We had spent so much time trying to recruit Family Medicine to join us, some six months, that we hadn't tried to recruit any permanent physicians. In retrospect this was not very smart on our part. This would have to be a top priority now.

CHAPTER 9

FINANCIAL STRUGGLE

Our district's tax income was based on a mil levy, a percentage of the town tax monies collected. This was structured such that the district received a monthly stipend, with the first payment being received in March when the first tax money came in for the year. Inasmuch as the greatest tax income was generated in the early part of the year, the disbursement to us was greatest at this time of year. Thereafter, our monthly tax income diminished such that by early fall it became miniscule and then dwindled to nothing. Our budget had to anticipate this period of famine, roughly from October to March each year.

As mentioned earlier, the head of our finance committee, Dave Bohl, had indicated at the September board meeting that it would be "nip and tuck" for us to be able to meet our budget to year end. He had suggested that the board request a $50,000 line-of-credit from the Dr. Mary Fisher Foundation to tide us over until the next tax monies would become available.

This foundation had an interesting history in itself. Dr. Mary Fisher had been the first physician to reside in Pagosa, coming on the scene early in the twentieth century after having

Dr. Mary Fisher

graduated from medical school in Chicago. She had to have been a rugged woman to practice in this mountain area, traveling on horseback to visit sick patients out in the backcountry. She had married, but she had no children.

The Dr. Mary Fisher Foundation had been named after her. The Foundation had originally built the Dr. Mary Fisher Medical Center (clinic) in 1996 using private funds and a bond issue passed by the citizenry. For several reasons, including poor management, this project foundered, and the foundation ended up selling the property and the building to the Upper San Juan Health Service District (USJHSD or simply district). The State of Colorado had established special districts with their own set of State laws to cover public utilities and the like, such as public health service, water, parks, and hospitals. Established in the early '80s as a special district, the USJHSD in Pagosa Springs had then contained only the EMS or Emergency Medical Service. The monies the foundation received from the sale, plus investment income, were to be used solely to support the health service district. In addition, over the years they received private donations to help build up their reservoir of funds. The foundation board worked closely with the health district board to help out in financial predicaments like the present one.

Bob Goodman, a well-known local businessman from a family that had lived in the area for six generations, and I sat on the foundation board as representatives from the health district board. Bob presented our request for funds and a plan for repayment. We explained our present financial predicament, how it had arisen largely from the debt we had inherited from the previous administration, and how we still had a large drain on our income from the money-losing clinic situation. They wanted to know how we were going to solve the clinic problem. We informed them of our failed efforts to merge with the Family Medicine Clinic and its failure. We told them that we were still working on solving this problem but, as yet, we had no clear solution. The latter did not sit well with them but they were otherwise very sympathetic. We indicated that repayment would begin in March, when tax funds started coming in, with the final payment to be made in June. They were very understanding and gave us the $50,000 line-of-credit.

CHAPTER 10

TASMANIA

Through the summer and fall, Jim Knoll and I had lunch at the DQ about every two weeks. These meetings with Jim were very helpful for me. Though Jim wasn't on the board, he attended all of our meetings and was up-to-date on all our proceedings. He was a knowledgeable and active audience participant in discussions on all our policy matters. As I mentioned previously, Jim had encountered many of the district's past problems in his pre-retirement work with the Presbyterian Health Care System in Dallas, Texas. This experience had paid off in spades for us, best exemplified by the election results. Now we were seeing the fruit borne from the personnel he had chosen as board and committee members, a group who worked hard and well together with virtually no divisiveness.

Jim was planning on spending six months in Tasmania as a *locum* psychiatrist, leaving in the latter part of October and returning in early May. So now I was picking his brain, getting his opinion on everything that might be of help while he was away: finances, policies, and thoughts about the clinic situation. Because he would be away during the negotiations, Jim had not been placed on the *ad hoc* Planning Committee to negotiate with Dr. Jim Pruitt and his group.

The clinic had been on Jim Knoll's mind, and he had encouraged the negotiations between Family Medicine and the finance committee even though he was pessimistic and thought the negotiations would fail. He encouraged our new talks with Jim Pruitt, but he admitted to a lack of confidence that they would be any more successful than the prior talks. Previously he hadn't given me his real thoughts about the clinic, not wanting to sabotage the earlier talks underway. But now he revealed to me what he really thought on this subject. Deep-down, Jim felt that the town did not need more than one clinic. Family Medicine was a thriving, profitable private clinic. Why should we persist in supporting a public clinic that had always been a money-loser? It was an unneeded duplication of services.

Our clinic had an emergency room, but so did Family Medicine. Our *locum* physicians sent most emergencies on to Mercy Hospital in Durango without treating them other than to stabilize them, while Jim Pruitt and his group provided more extensive on-site ER services such as setting simple fractures and sewing up lacerations. Our clinic saw all patients and never turned away a patient because of finances, but Jim's group did the same even though they lost money by doing so. Our clinic provided no service that wasn't being done better by Family Medicine; and, to boot, they did it profitably.

I told Jim that the townspeople would be upset by the closing of "their" clinic, which they supported with their tax money. Also, what would we do with an empty clinic building?

Jim mentioned that those were the two arguments that had kept him quiet to this point. Also, he mentioned that he was only stating this to me, and he didn't think it would do any good to make his view public now. He still had hopes that Family Medicine and our clinic would merge, which would be the best solution.

Jim thought that we were doing everything possible to solve our financial problems, and that this would improve with time. We just needed to be patient and continue to pay down debt. We hated to see Jim leave, but fortunately he would still be available by email.

CHAPTER 11

LOAN REDUX

By late November we had used up a good portion of the line-of-credit we had received from the Dr. Mary Fisher Foundation. It became clear that the funds we had borrowed would fall far short of the money needed to survive until the first tax funds became available in March, but we knew we couldn't go back to the foundation for another loan.

The next logical source for funds would be our bank, Citizen's Bank of Pagosa Springs, for a similar line-of-credit. The board delegated Pam, our chairwoman, Bob Goodman, our treasurer, and our district manager, Allan Hughes, to make this request. Whereas we had only asked the foundation for $50,000, we were now being more realistic and asking the bank for a $200,000 line-of-credit. Again, repayment would begin when the first tax monies were received in March. One factor that had made our situation worse was that the clinic patient load, and thus income, fell considerably in the fall because there were few tourists, and tourists were a main source for clinic income. The tourist traffic would pick up in the winter with the ski crowd arriving, but the period from the time of billing to the reception of payments was several months so this wouldn't help us in the winter months before the March tax money became available.

The bank was very supportive and gave us the line-of-credit. We breathed a sigh of relief, another problem solved at least temporarily.

CHAPTER 12

A NEW CLINIC IDEA

Our planning committee reported to the board that they, too, had failed to come to an agreement with Family Medicine about merging the two clinics. At that time I requested that our *ad hoc* committee be continued with a new purpose, that of finding another solution to the clinic problem. The committee members would remain the same, namely Jerry Valade, J.R. Ford, Dave Bohl, and me. The board concurred. Jerry had recovered from his pneumonia by mid-fall. I had asked him on his return to the committee if he would like to resume being head of the committee. He deferred, letting me continue to head the committee. Now that we were no longer meeting with Jim Pruitt, both Jerry and I could be on the committee without breaking the "Sunshine Law." We continued to meet every two weeks thereafter.

By the end of January the *locum* physician contracts were to expire, and they were asking in December whether or not their contracts would be renewed. We were aware of just two options at this time: renew their contracts or close the clinic. We were all averse to closing the clinic, and the *locum* physicians were amenable to renewing their contracts for a shorter term of three months. So, that's what we did. It bought us a little more time to make other plans.

At this time we began looking for a physician or group that could be brought in to jump-start our clinic after the *locum* physicians' contracts expired at the end of April. First, we talked to Dr. Don Bader, head of the ER group at Mercy Hospital in Durango, about manning our clinic with one of their ER docs. Actually, they could rotate the docs so they wouldn't be sacrificing the same doc to us full-time. They considered this, but in the end they said no. They may have been too thinly staffed to afford having one of their docs gone five days a week. More likely, they didn't want to get involved in a practice that was outside their specialty area of emergency medicine.

Another possibility was to ask an out-of-town physician group to man our clinic. We talked to an interested group in Durango, but they eventually said no, too. The 60-mile distance between the towns and the competition from Family Medicine probably turned them off.

Then, another possibility appeared out of the blue. A physician from Dallas who was considering moving to Pagosa visited Dr. Pruitt's Family Medicine Clinic, looking for a practice opportunity. Dan Keunig, Family Medicine's nurse practitioner, told me about him, and I obtained his name and telephone number. I figured it would not hurt to talk to him.

Dr. Ken Patterson responded to my call. He was presently working as an ER physician in a hospital just outside Dallas, and he was now in negotiations to swap his home in Texas for one in Pagosa. In addition to practicing medicine, he was considering opening an art gallery in Pagosa with the same person with whom he was going to swap homes. A further impetus for his moving to and practicing in the Pagosa area was his desire, like mine had been, to live in the mountains of Colorado and be able to hike and ski nearby. He was returning to Pagosa shortly, so we set up an appointment to meet.

I had lunch with Ken Patterson a week or so later. We met at the Hogsbreath, a western-style eating establishment popular to the locals as well as tourists, specializing in steaks and barbecue. Tall and slim with a short beard and red hair, Ken's forbearers could have been Vikings. He spoke softly with a quiet and thoughtful demeanor.

Ken, formerly a family physician, had switched to practicing emergency medicine several years earlier. He indicated that he and his wife, also a family physician, had practiced together for about a dozen years until she opted to stay home and care for their seven kids and do home schooling. Now she was interested in doing some part-time practice to hone her medical skills.

Ken was considering joining Jim Pruitt's practice, but he wasn't sure he wanted to return to family medicine, particularly full-time. I queried whether he would be interested in helping us set up a new clinic. He said he would consider the possibility. However, he wanted to spend some time in setting up and running his new art gallery, too. On moving to Pagosa, which seemed almost certain by this time with the house swap about completed, he planned on flying back to Dallas every month to continue his ER work there until he had a secure position in the Pagosa area.

At our next planning committee meeting I told the members about Dr. Patterson. They were all interested in what possibilities this might open up for us. My thinking then was to make Ken the medical director and have him practice in the clinic part-time, thereby giving him some time to work in his art gallery. I knew of other docs in the area who were working part-time who might be able to work us into their schedules as well. Initially we would need just one doc on duty at a time for a five-day week. That same doc could be on night call, thus providing 24/5 coverage during the week. When the patient load increased, we could then consider increasing physician coverage and extending coverage to the weekends. I thought this plan stood a reasonable chance of success, and the planning committee agreed.

On his next visit to Pagosa, Ken met with the planning committee. The interview went well, and the committee members were impressed with him. We then sought board approval to negotiate a contract with Ken to set up and work in the clinic and to become the new medical director. The board gave its approval, and Jerry began negotiations.

In the meantime, I began contacting physicians in the community who might be interested in working with us on a part-time basis in the clinic. Of course, all of this would occur on setting up a new clinic after our *locum* physicians' contracts expired.

Dr. Bob Brown, the physician who had worked half-time in the old Dr. Mary Fisher Clinic when they had resigned in toto, now some two years ago, had continued his Trinidad ER work half-time but had also opened a part-time boutique practice (pay-as-you-go and not accepting any insurance) in Pagosa. Bob was interested in working with us and indicated that he could give us one day a week.

I then contacted Carol, a family doc who had recently resigned from working in the Indian Clinic down in Arboles, in the southwest part of our county. She was interested in giving us one day a week, also. She wanted more time with her family so this fit well into her schedule. She was particularly interested in pediatrics and women's health, which would be an asset for us.

Another family physician, Nancy, had worked part-time at the Dr. Mary Fisher Clinic in the past and had a good reputation with the local docs. She was working part-time in Durango now. She was also interested in giving us one day of work per week. She, like Carol, wanted to spend more time with her family.

I had continued to talk to Dr. Don Bader at Mercy Emergency, and he indicated now that they might be able to spare one of their ER docs one day a week as well.

I contacted one of our *locum* docs who lived in Durango. When his contract with us expired in March, he was planning on setting up his own practice in Durango but he could give us one day a week, too, like the other docs.

Until the end of 2004 our clinic had employed a nurse practitioner out of Durango who covered the clinic one day a week. He had been let go in December because of the lack of business, so I presented our plan to him and found him interested in giving us a day a week also.

Dr. Patterson said that he could give us two days of clinic work and then spend one day a week as medical director, attending to the administrative duties of the position. All of these physicians were agreeable to covering for a 24-hour period, eight hours on duty in the clinic and then covering off-site for sixteen hours, thus giving us the 24/5 coverage for the weekdays and nights that we had been seeking. So, it was clear that we had more than an ample number of physicians to man the clinic. I had little doubt that we could obtain a supporting staff on short notice, also.

We looked at our budget and produced a financial model that appeared workable. In fact, it cut the physician expenses, compared to the *locum* physicians' salaries, by about a third while still maintaining night coverage. All of these physicians were known in the community, except for Ken. We anticipated that this would help us build up a good practice within a reasonable period of time, but realistically it might take as long as a year to break even. The citizens of Pagosa would now have a chance to build up a long-standing relationship with their physician of choice at both clinics.

By now, having learned my lesson, I felt I must check Ken's past records. His medical credentials were fine, and he had already applied for his Colorado medical license. In the several meetings I had with Ken, I came away with the feeling that he was a solid citizen, a good physician, and a fine family man. I hadn't met his wife, Sheila, but anyone who bore seven children, then gave up her medical practice to care for them and then home school them must be a pretty fine individual. In Ken, I thought we could hardly have gotten a better candidate for this position.

The only reservation I had about our clinic setup was that all the physicians would be working part-time. Would the physician on duty be able to cover the other physicians' patients sufficiently well? Would the patients, themselves, be satisfied with their physician being available just one day a week? This arrangement would be satisfactory to get us off the ground, but I did see the need to have one full-time physician eventually. Then the part-time physicians could fill in nicely. I did wonder if having Ken just being part-time would hurt us. It would have been nice if he had been able to work full-time in the clinic, at the same time being the medical director.

CHAPTER 13

A SEISMIC SHIFT

At the board meeting in March we met in executive session with Jim Pruitt and his entire Family Medicine physician group. This was a non-public meeting because we would be discussing whether or not to renew the *locum* physician contracts which were expiring at the end of the next month. We were going to make one final attempt to work something out with Family Medicine, Jim Pruitt and his group, to man our clinic.

Our discussion did not go well. Jim and his partners proposed a plan wherein they would cover our clinic from 4-8 pm daily, five days a week, the only hours it would be open. However, there would not be a physician in-house. Rather, they would have one of their staff at our facility to screen the patients that came in. If a patient needed to see a physician, he or she would be sent over to the Family Medicine building next door. In essence they suggested extending their work hours while taking our patients. We would have no medical practice in our building, no income, and to boot we would have to pay them for the coverage. Closing the clinic, putting a sign on the door and telling patients to go next door would have the same effect and would have cost us nothing. I thought their offer was insulting, though I didn't say so. I believe they felt that we were desperate enough to take any deal.

No one on our board took their offer seriously. Our planning committee was still in negotiations with Dr. Patterson and the other docs concerning their taking over the clinic. However, it was clear that a change to the new physician staff for the clinic could not be accomplished until late June at the earliest, so that left a hiatus of two months with the *locum* docs' contracts expiring at the end of April. The new physicians we would employee had prior commitments, and this was the earliest they would be available.

We considered renewing the *locum* physician contracts again. However, no one really wanted to keep perpetuating a failed, money-losing situation. Of course, the only other alternative was to close the clinic.

My thought was that closing the clinic for a couple months would not be bad if we could then reopen shortly thereafter with the new staff. I felt that we could probably retain most of the support staff for this short period until we reopened.

We had a lively discussion on these alternatives. Finally, one of the board members made the motion to close the clinic. We had further discussion, with board members feeling strongly on both sides of the issue. However, the only way we could stay open without a break in coverage was to rehire the *locum* physicians. We had delayed making a decision in December and had rehired the *locum* physicians then for another three months. Were we going to repeat this costly course in perpetuity?

The vote was four to close, including myself, and three opposed. We had done what none of us had ever wanted to do. I knew that we "aye voters" felt a deep sense of responsibility for what we had done. I know that I did. However, at that time I presumed that we would be up and operational in several months with the new clinic. Otherwise, I don't believe that I would have voted to close the clinic. We knew that we would draw some flack from the townspeople for closing "their" clinic.

CHAPTER 14

CLOSER TO REALITY

Sheldon Weisgrau, the consultant whom we hired to do the feasibility study for a critical access hospital, presented his findings at a special board meeting in May. The meeting had been advertised in the *Pagosa Springs Sun*, and we had a large crowd in attendance. Sheldon had constructed two models, one showing a slow growth pattern in hospitalized patients and the other a more rapid growth model. The weaker model would have us break even financially within a year, and the more aggressive one would show a profit in the same time frame. He emphasized the importance of our local physicians being willing to hospitalize patients in the new facility rather than referring them to Mercy Hospital in Durango as they did presently. Of course, the latter was their only choice now.

The board and public had a slew of questions, all of which Sheldon handled easily and positively. I believe it was to clear to everyone that this was the right time to take this big step and build a CAH in Pagosa Springs. Our population was growing rapidly, and we should be able to obtain the funds. The CAH would allow us to catch up and would be an integral part of finally being able to provide twenty-first century healthcare for our populace.

Everyone felt positive about the report and looked forward to determining our next step in this project. Now we had the task of considering how large a hospital was practical and what we could afford. These were queries for which we had no immediate answer, but we now had a clear path to follow.

Later, on reflection, I felt that we getting a handle on our finances with the tax money now coming in, our loans and other debts were being paid down, and we finally had a plausible solution for the clinic if we followed our present course. Now, it looked like our vision for a critical access hospital and all our hard work was finally paying off.

CHAPTER 15

THE GURU RETURNS

In mid-May Dr. Jim Knoll returned from his *locum* physician sojourn to Tasmania. When he went over, he hadn't been quite sure what his position there would be. As it turned out, he was temporarily replacing a prison psychiatrist. He had written me a week or so after he had started work and said that in his first week he had evaluated both a serial killer and a serial rapist. It was a new experience. I am not sure how much he enjoyed the work experience. However, he said that he and wife Ingrid did enjoy the island with its wonderful variety of flora and fauna.

While in Tasmania, Jim's artistic and talented wife, Ingrid, had sent us a clever Christmas card which she had drawn depicting Jim in prison garb, wearing a cowboy hat with a tassel, standing behind bars with the inscription, "Greetings from Risdon Prison." It was hysterical. We framed it and it still sits on a table in my office.

Jim and I had lunch at the DQ shortly after his return. I brought him up-to-date on the events that had transpired since his departure. He was happy to hear of Sheldon's positive report on the CAH, and he too thought it would likely be a go. He agreed with our having closed the clinic. He was glad that we would finally be able to stop the money drain.

Jim felt less certain about reopening the clinic, as I had proposed. He still thought it would be a money-losing proposition. I told him about Ken, the plan to have him work in the clinic part-time and be the medical director plus having other physicians in town work part-time in the clinic.

By this time Ken and his family had moved to Pagosa Springs. He had leased space which was presently under renovation for the art gallery that would open in the summer. Ken continued to fly back and forth to Dallas to cover his ER practice there.

Jim, Ken and I had lunch at a new restaurant in town about a week later. As it turned out, the restaurant had a nice atmosphere, but unfortunately the food wasn't very good. We passed a few pleasantries, Ken telling Jim about his family and move. While this was going on, I thought the inferior food had set a poor mood. In recent years I had come to feel that events often happened synergistically for better or worse. I had read Joseph Jaworski's book, *Synchronicity: The Inner Path of Leadership*,[18] not long before and agreed with the author that good and opportune events often occurred together and vice versa.

So, I did not feel good about our meeting and felt uncomfortable. To me, the atmosphere felt strained.

Ken and I detailed the plans for the new clinic and the personnel involved. Jim said little. I recalled his statement from the previous fall when he had said he thought it would be best to close the district's public clinic because it only duplicated the better run and profitable private clinic in town. At that time he had not wanted to state this publicly, so I did not raise the subject now with Ken present. But I wondered if this was not the thought foremost in Jim's mind now. Time would tell if this was so.

Our luncheon wound down and just petered out—pretty much a dud.

CHAPTER 16

HEART REVISITED

As related previously, I had been going downhill physically for several years, which I had originally attributed to aging. Then in March 2004 I discovered my heart valve degeneration problem, for which I had open-heart surgery. That was certainly a major occurrence in my life. My recovery had been much slower than I had anticipated, but then I really didn't know to what extent I would recover. My surgeon indicated that I would recover in six weeks. It wasn't until later that I realized that he only meant recovery from the surgery and not from the underlying heart problem. My post-op electrocardiogram and echocardiogram showed that I had residual damage to the left ventricle of my heart, but I presumed that I would feel significantly better because the mitral regurgitation was no longer present. Before surgery the blood flow resulted in 50 percent of the blood being ejected normally from the left ventricle into the aorta, while the other 50 percent regurgitated backwards up into the left atrium from whence it had come. Now all the blood was going forward so the left ventricle was now pumping out almost twice the blood it had before surgery. That should make me feel stronger and give me more aerobic capacity and thus a better exercise capacity. I didn't really feel that much better than I had just before surgery. Why?

In my early days of medical practice and in academic medicine at the University of Maryland Medical Center, I had done research wherein I had developed a computer model of the cardio-respiratory system. In so doing I had become versed in flow dynamics, i.e., flow rates, pressures and volumes in pipes which could be equated to blood flow and pressures in the heart and blood vessels.

At my surgery the middle third of the posterior leaflet of the mitral valve had been found to be degenerated, and it had been resected. The two remaining sides were then sutured together. The leaflet was now one-third smaller and too small to close the mitral orifice, along with the normal anterior leaflet, when the left ventricle contracted. If the surgeon had left it this way, I would still have had mitral regurgitation. To correct this deficiency, he had inserted a plastic ring around the mitral orifice, which made the opening smaller. This better accommodated the reduced size of the posterior leaflet, and in effect stopped any significant backward flow or regurgitation.

However, the ring produced a smaller opening between the left atrium and ventricle, which resulted in a reduced blood flow between the two chambers.

Inasmuch as the right side of the heart contracts and pushes blood through the lungs and over to the left side of the heart, it is necessary for the left heart to pump out the same amount of blood. Otherwise the lungs would become congested, resulting in left-sided congestive heart failure. To prevent this scenario, the surgeon placed a similar ring on the right side of the heart in the tricuspid valve orifice between the right atrium and ventricle. Reducing the blood flow from right to left, commensurate with the output from the left side of the heart, would keep everything in balance.

Just before surgery my ejection fraction (volume/pressure) from the left ventricle was a normal 70 percent, even with the 50 percent mitral regurgitation. Several echos after the surgery showed the ejection fraction to be 40 percent, a significant reduction. I presumed that this resulted primarily from the introduction of the two smaller rings into the two valve orifices and not so much from any damage to the left ventricular muscle. Otherwise, how could one explain the reduction in the ejection fraction from 70 percent before surgery to 40 percent afterwards?

This was not explained to me before surgery. My surgeon had explained pre-op that we had a choice of the procedure he had done versus replacing the mitral valve with a synthetic one. If he had done the latter, then I would have to remain on anticoagulants for the rest of my life as thrombi, blood clots, could form on the synthetic valve, break off, and go into the circulation causing a stroke. I had opted for the more conservative procedure.

If I had known about the reduced flow dynamics from the procedure beforehand, I believe I would have opted for the synthetic valve, inasmuch as I most likely would have had a better exercise capacity. There would have been no need to insert rings to reduce the size of the orifices. Being a health nut and an exercise enthusiast, the ability to run, hike and ski had always been an important part of my life. I had accommodated to slowing down, thinking it was an aging effect; but if I had a chance to get back what I had lost, I would have picked the synthetic valve.

Now I was relegated to moving much slower. My kind wife would go with me, but I could no longer keep up with her or with our hiking and skiing friends in our Outdoor Club. I tried my best, but my best now was less than half of what I could do several years before.

I do not know whether my surgeon realized the effect this procedure would have on my exercise capacity or whether he realized it would make any difference to me. Perhaps he felt that at my age of 74 I should be happy with what turned out to be my end result. It was clear that without the surgery I would have gone into heart failure in the not-too-distant future. I am sure he felt that the more conservative procedure was the correct one, and I can't fault him for his rationale.

CHAPTER 17

THE PAIN OF PROGRESS

As the year progressed, the board as a whole was becoming somewhat disenchanted with the performance of our district manager, Allan Hughes. To a large degree this revolved around financial matters. We were deeply in debt for most of the year. We had needed the lines-of-credit from both the Dr. Mary Fisher Foundation and Citizen's Bank, and these were being paid off on time. By mid-year we should be clear of this debt. We had been depending on the tax money coming in starting in March, and that had worked out as planned. I thought that Allan had managed our finances quite well.

However, there were two main areas of concern. The first was the format for the presentation of our monthly financial reports and an explanation of our finances. The board had delegated to the finance committee the job of preparing a format that would be concise, clear and understandable for all board members. Four of the board members were businessmen, and it seemed that each had a different idea on how this format should be accomplished. I presumed that each wanted to see a report similar to what they each used in their own businesses. So, with each presentation of a new financial model someone was unhappy with the format, which resulted in the finance committee having to go back to the drawing board to come up with a new model. Allan worked with the finance committee on these successive models. When the board asked Allan for a detailed explanation of different financial aspects of the report, they at times found him wanting. Myself, I thought that Allan handled these queries quite well.

I didn't have as much financial background as the businessmen on the board and on our finance committee, but neither was I a neophyte. I had always used a hands-on approach for the business in my medical practice. So, even though I may have had something to offer in this area, I pretty much stayed out of this fray.

I had no doubt that we had the expertise to develop a good financial report. This may seem to be too small a matter to take up this much time, but our financial status was so precarious, we all wanted every detail to be clear so we wouldn't miss any worsening situation. If Allan had been more financially adept, he probably would have been all right. When we hired Allan, we knew his background was in emergency medicine and not business or finance. So, it should not have come as a surprise to anyone to see that we got exactly what we had bargained for, expertise in the area of his training and experience. Under the circumstances, I thought Allan had done a good job. After all, we did have a finance committee to help him out. In fact, that may have been part of the problem, having four strong financial experts on the committee doing the work that overlapped the jurisdiction of the district manager. In the end, one of our board members, Bob Scott, showed us a format used by the Mercy Hospital Board. This was modified to meet our needs and became our monthly financial report to everyone's satisfaction.

Another criticism was that Allan had not been forthcoming in planning for the district's future. I had talked to Allan about this half-way through the year. He commented that he didn't know what the board expected of him and indicated that he was getting mixed signals from various board members. He felt that there was no way he could make everyone happy. He didn't know what to do and almost felt like giving up at this point.

We did have a strong board and every member contributed to our on-going progress. It was clear that it would take a strong and experienced manager to satisfy everyone's expectations. For his part, Allan worked long hours and tried to give the board what he perceived they wanted. He had played a principal part in fashioning our return to solvency, which was our number one goal for this first year.

We were now moving into a new era, which would require a CEO with both expertise and experience in building and operating the new critical access hospital. We had, in fact, turned down a candidate with just this experience the year before because his income request exceeded our salary cap. Instead, we had hired Allan who was within this cap. I believe that Allan fulfilled his mission for our first year, but now it was clear that we needed another type of person to carry us into the future, someone with hospital experience. I was in favor of replacing Allan, too, even though I felt guilty in doing so. I had been a staunch supporter of Allan just a year ago when we hired him. I did tell him that I thought he had done a good job.

CHAPTER 18

MERCY: A PLAN ACCOMPLISHED

One of the original tenants in the "Position Statement" that we adopted when we ran for election was to develop a closer relationship with Mercy Hospital in Durango. As mentioned previously, several of us had talked to the head of emergency services, and also the CEO of Mercy Hospital in Durango the previous year, and they both had declined to become involved with our health district until there was a change in the board and administration. In early spring one of our board members, Bob Scott, began talking to Mercy's chief operations officer (COO) about their becoming involved in our present and future planning. Then in May our chairwoman, Pam Hopkins, indicated that Mercy had contacted her about making a presentation to our board on how they might be able to help us as we moved forward. This was placed on the agenda for our May meeting. I was happy to see that this item in our original Six Point Plan was now likely to come true.

Four Mercy executives, including their CEO and COO, attended our board meeting, and they made an excellent PowerPoint presentation. In essence, their plan would place one of their executives on one of our committees to advise us on whatever matters were of concern to us. It was a simple plan, and all board members liked the idea. However, there was one item that was disturbing to me. Mercy wanted to place one of their executives in our district manager's position, which, to me, meant giving them too much control over our administrative affairs. I did not question this point in the public session as I knew that we would be going into a private, executive session immediately following this meeting. That would be a better venue to argue this point.

Allan Hughes's contract would expire at the end of June. As I mentioned previously, the board did not feel that he would be the best person to lead us into the future. Mercy obviously knew that we were looking for a new district manager when they recommended one of their own for this position.

As soon as the executive session began, Dr. Jim Pruitt brought up the same point that I was going to argue. We both felt that our new district manager should be independent of Mercy. Both Jim and I were happy to have Mercy act in a consultative capacity, especially in the planning for the CAH, but there were several reasons for feeling that they shouldn't have control of our administration. One point that bothered both Jim and me was that the Mercy administration, themselves, and their docs had been at loggerheads for sometime now. I didn't know the details but was aware that this was, at least in part, financial. In fact, a group of the docs had left Mercy, formed a separate group, and built their own Doctor's Hospital in Durango. This obviously happened because there was a serious and unresolved rift between the two parties. Some years back Mercy had employed the docs with disastrous consequences, resulting in a huge financial loss in their unwinding themselves from that situation. Perhaps this experience played a part in their reticence now to come to an agreement with the docs. This fact made me feel uncomfortable giving this much power to an outside group with whom we had no track record.

Another and perhaps a more obvious reason was that Mercy's interest in helping us had to revolve around their own self-interest. We were an area that referred a large number of patients to them. It made sense for them to become involved in our hospital plans to protect their referral base. If push came to shove, I felt they would always favor their own self-interest over ours. To serve as our consultant, yes, but to serve as our head administrator, no, was my strong feeling.

The final negative was that their man for the DM position would give us just 80 percent of his time at what would be almost double the salary Allan was presently receiving. He would maintain his position at Mercy, working there 20 percent of the time. I had seen this type of division of labor before, and I knew that he would too easily devote more of his time to his primary job at Mercy where his performance by his superiors would be judged. By contract, he would be giving us 80 percent of a 40-hour week (that is, 32 hours a week). I knew that Allan had frequently given us much more than 40 hours per week, up to 70 hours on some occasions. So, with this limitation I was dubious that progress would be maintained at a good pace.

Another point came to mind that I brought up but which had little impact. Mercy was a large general hospital. What we in Pagosa Springs were contemplating was a small rural critical access hospital. I felt it would make more sense to hire someone now who had experience in setting up such a hospital. There were 25 CAH's in Colorado from which to draw an experienced executive in exactly the area we needed. Why not tap this pool of talent?

I had just been to a critical access hospital conference in Breckinridge, Colorado, and had spoken with many of the administrators of CAH's. They were a different animal with different problems and solutions than seen in large hospitals. At this meeting I met several experienced executives who expressed interest in helping us become a CAH. We were in a rapidly growing area, a beautiful resort town, and we were developing a new medical complex, certainly an attractive position for a young, experienced administrator. An executive at one of these hospitals who had just helped another CAH out of dire financial difficulties elaborated how he had done this in a very creative and innovative way. Best of all, he was telling me about it after the plan had been implemented and had been successful. So, I recommended that we talk to this individual for the DM, and eventually CEO, position. This was all to no avail. The majority of the board was set on going entirely with Mercy.

We further debated Mercy providing us with a district manager, but it was clear that Jim Pruitt and I were fighting a losing battle. A motion was made to accept the Mercy proposal in its entirety, including their providing our district manager. The motion passed by a five-to-two margin, Jim Pruitt and I being the dissenters.

This episode gave me the feeling that the majority of our new board felt insecure and not yet up to the job of leading the way, but rather wanted someone else to share the leadership. In this case, in my judgment, we were giving away too much responsibility.

It had been a difficult year, but I felt that we had done very well considering the circumstances. Finances and the clinic had been our dominant problems, and both were looking better now. I didn't doubt that the Mercy group could help us with our finances, but they could do this on a consultative basis rather than by "running the show." I felt that the clinic situation was being resolved. However, I didn't doubt that the Mercy group would also have some input into the clinic plan.

Earlier in the year I had read a book by John Carver, *Boards That Make a Difference: A New Design for Leadership in Non-profit and Public Organizations.*[17] It was about public and corporate boards, how they often functioned and how they should function. It was clear that new board members usually act very conservatively, as they should, during the learning process. It usually takes at least a year and often two years before a new board member feels comfortable and confident in making decisions, especially in a leadership role. This was such a good read for where we were that I bought a copy of the book for each board member. It advises that new board members should be educated by the experienced members even before they take office and then coached along the way. Unfortunately, we had come on board as all new members. I had a year experience, but for the most part I was fighting battles for that year so I can't say that I learned much about parliamentary procedure and board governance. What I did do was get experience by talking to board members and executives in other areas of Colorado, including Telluride, Del Norte, Alamosa, and Breckenridge. This helped me gain confidence in what I was doing and what I proposed. I do not know how many board directors read the book. No one commented to me that they had other than Pam, our chairwoman. My thinking now was that our board still felt insecure about making major decisions that would have long-term effects. Letting Mercy, with their obvious experience, share the leadership was the conservative approach, and I cannot say it was wrong. But at this time I did not feel the need for as much guidance as did the other board members. Time would judge the wisdom of letting Mercy control our administration.

A week after our last session the same Mercy executives conducted a workshop for the board to prioritize our main areas of interest. Each board member made a list of what they thought were the 12 most important areas that needed to be dealt with by the district. These were then graded according to our levels of concern. To no one's surprise, our number one concern was our finances. Second and third were also predictable: the clinic and the critical access hospital. This gave the Mercy execs an indication of our primary concerns and where they and our new district manager needed to concentrate their efforts.

Rick O'Block, a mild-mannered, well-spoken executive, became our new district manager from Mercy. He overlapped with Allan for two weeks to smooth the transition. Rick grasped the financial situation readily and thereafter continued to pay down our debt. This was made easier now that the clinic was closed and no longer a drain on our resources. The tax money coming in, along with the income from EMS and the outstanding clinic receipts, were more than enough to care for any debt incurred by EMS and to handle the line-of-credit debt repayment. However, the collection agency to which we had outsourced our clinic and EMS billing was doing an extremely poor job, and this needed immediate attention. This was an area in which Rick was familiar, and he set about correcting this trouble spot.

CHAPTER 19

END OF AN ERA

It early June, our planning committee decided that we would not be ready to reopen the clinic in late June with so much work still to do, so the opening was postponed until mid-July, which seemed reasonable. Our committee presented this new opening date to the board at the June meeting. Now there was hesitation regarding reopening the clinic at all. It was on everyone's mind that we would be returning to a money-losing situation at least for a while. After the disastrous, money-losing clinic debacle of the past year, no one wanted a repetition of what had been the prime cause for our fiscal woes. But to waver now was disconcerting to me after all the careful planning. I wondered if the Mercy group had added their voice to this decision-making process. After discussion, the board tabled making any decision on reopening the clinic at this time, an ominous sign for the clinic plan but understandable from a fiscal standpoint.

After Sheldon Weisgrau's glowing CAH report in May, we had passed a motion to go ahead with plans to build a critical access hospital. I was ecstatic about this decision. I found myself anxious to get started on this project. I was the only member on the grants committee now, as Tom Steen had previously resigned as head of this committee because of our inaction in applying for grants in the prior year. This was due to the fact that we didn't have any set plans for our future to support grant requests. Most of the year was spent waiting for the consultant's report on going forward with a CAH, solving the clinic problem, and paying down debt.

I knew there was grant money available, particularly from the Colorado Mineral and Energy Fund, in the amount of about $500,000. The deadline for submitting a grant was August 1; otherwise the next deadline was November 1. I saw no reason to not go ahead with the submission. I obtained the application and contacted the representative of DOLA, the Colorado Department of Local Affairs, in Durango, who would be on the committee that would decide grant recipients. He agreed to help us prepare the grant. However, I needed board approval before engaging in all the work required in this effort. The board did not give approval, and no one gave a clear reason for this rejection. I was disappointed, but I did not press for an explanation.

Later, in retrospect, I realized that I was so gung-ho on getting the ball rolling on the critical access hospital that I was literally trying to pull the board along in the direction I wanted to go. I think my passion may have gotten the better of my reasoning. I believe my fellow board members were sympathetic but weren't about to make a hasty decision, particularly when the availability of the grant money was not going away. The infrastructure and detailed plans for going ahead with the CAH had not yet been laid, and this was necessary to prevent any mistakes in what was to be the largest project ever undertaken by the USJHSD.

Later in June, the planning committee for the new clinic was dissolved. In its place a new *ad hoc* committee, The Critical Access Hospital Pathway Committee, was established to work with Mercy in planning for the CAH. I was placed on the new committee along with Drs. Jim Knoll and Jim Pruitt and two businessmen, Dave Bohl and J.R. Ford from the finance committee. The committee also included a representative from the Mercy Hospital group. Several days later our chairwoman, Pam, called me and said that "they" felt that there were too many docs on the committee and would I mind if she removed me from the committee. What could I say? "Sure!" That left a bitter taste in my mouth. It seemed like I was being relegated to the sidelines.

The termination of the planning committee put a finis to the reopening of the clinic. It had suffered a slow death, ending with hardly a whimper. Its future was not to be discussed formally at a board meeting but rather left to die, our resuscitation efforts for the clinic having failed. I understood the fear of restarting the clinic and again incurring the losses that had so hampered our getting out of debt. I also understood that debating the issue at a public meeting would unnecessarily bring the issue to the public's attention, something that was not desirable inasmuch as the public had already accepted the clinic's closure.

A year later, Jim Knoll told me that he had lobbied against reopening the clinic with the board members, his rationale being the same as he had mentioned to me previously: we had no reason to replicate a profitable, private clinic with a money-losing public clinic. Of course, this was the strongest argument of all and obviously put the final nail in the public clinic's coffin.

At this later time, I also realized that the critical access hospital would incorporate the Dr. Mary Fisher Clinic building into its plan, thus negating the argument that might come from the public that we had closed "their" clinic without making any plans for its future.

Looking back over the past year I could see that, when the new board took control, we all had a common goal: focusing on getting out of our huge debt. But, as the year progressed, I could see where different factions on the board may have developed with somewhat different goals. In large part, I believe this was a matter of the new directors maturing and becoming more knowledgeable and confident in their decision-making prowess (board governance). Now they wanted to exert more control over our policy-making decisions. Thus, I think that a faction of the board, now re-enforced with Mercy group backing, was taking the lead in directing our forward progress. I don't believe this was devious behavior but rather represented a cyclical swing that occurs in the struggle for political power. Though I was unhappy about some of the recent decisions, I understood where they were coming from, their rationale, and that our board had "grown to adulthood," literally honed in the fires of adversity during the past year.

While all of this was going on my wife, Patti, was checking out places at lower altitude for us to eventually move. The oxygen saturation of my blood was running low, about 89-90 percent in the daytime. Normal saturation for this altitude of 7000 feet was 93 percent or higher. These daytime saturations were borderline normal. Below 90 percent was considered unhealthy and could lead to brain damage over the longer term. Also, at this level I felt short of breath on minimal exertion. Nevertheless, I continued to hike and ski with my wife but at a slower pace. Patti and I had talked many times about moving when we could no longer hike and ski in the mountains of Colorado. For me it looked like that time had come. For Patti, my health was her over-riding concern.

One day Patti came running into my home office proclaiming that she had found her "dream home" online. It was at less than 2000 feet elevation, the criterion one of my docs had recommended for obtaining a sufficient supply of oxygen. Would I fly out to Vancouver, Washington, with her to look at this home? I wasn't ready yet to take this step so I said no. Patti wasn't to be thwarted and asked if I minded if she asked her brother, Mike, to accompany her. I agreed that this was all right with me. Though Mike had just recently retired, I didn't think he would agree to go. After all, we all knew that it was a hobby of Patti's to enjoy house-hunting. However, Mike jumped at the opportunity and even offered to pay some of the expenses.

Two days later, on July 4, I received a call from Patti in Vancouver proclaiming that the house was even more wonderful than she had seen online. She felt I should come out immediately to look at it. She then put her brother Mike on the phone. He actually supported her in repeating that it was a great house and a good buy to boot. How could I say no? So, I drove down to Albuquerque, left our dog, Ghirardelli, with Mike's wife Helen, and caught a flight to Vancouver.

The next day we all looked at the home. I agreed that it was beautiful and the price was right. It was a mountain-type, Lindall cedar home set high on a small mountain with an expansive view of the Columbia River, about 1000 feet above sea level. I didn't like that it had three floors, since I felt that as we grew older we should live on just one floor to save our already battered knees. But I got pressured by both Patti and Mike. We all knew I would feel better at a lower altitude. In fact, we had gone to a lower elevation for a week on two occasions just to check out this premise. I clearly felt better at sea level, and I could be more active. I told them both that I would think about it. I knew that other people were looking at the home, as well, and that it could be bought out from under us if we delayed in making an offer. So, I gave myself 24 hours to think about it and to make up my mind. I knew that the only thing holding me back from moving was the obligation I felt to my fellow board members and my personal goal of not leaving Pagosa until my job with the district was finished. On the other hand, it was becoming abundantly clear that our board and committee members had matured. They had fought through hard times and now they could see the light at the end of the tunnel.

I could recall several occasions in my past when I had thought that I was indispensable in my work and would not let up, not even for the sake of going on vacation with my wife and friends. I had missed some great trips to Africa, the Galapagos Islands, and hiking in Switzerland and Austria, among others. Fortunately my wife made most of these trips, so at least I had not infected her with my delusion of being indispensable. So, I thought that this was likely another one of those times. Now, virtually everyone was making it clear that I was dispensable. Also, I knew that the board was unanimously set on going ahead with plans for the critical access hospital, so I wasn't needed to push that project any longer. It looked like I no longer had any battles to fight. The clinic battle was over, too. Was the war that Jim and I had been fighting over? Had we won? I concluded that we had, and it was time for this old foot soldier to retire. I acquiesced and agreed with Patti to buy the home in Vancouver and finally move out of the high altitude. Patti gave a sigh of relief.

We remained in Pagosa during the summer months and sold our home there easily, which allowed us to move to Vancouver by the end of August.

The district's new DM, Rick O'Block, continued to pay down our debt, and both lines-of-credit were paid off. Rick also started work on solving the billing/collection mess that had befallen us by choosing the wrong outsourcing company the year before. The new CAH committee was meeting and I presume making plans, but nothing had evolved as yet. The new relationship with the Mercy group appeared to be going well, too. So, it was a smooth transition to a new era, evolving from a year of debt-ridden clinic worries to one looking forward to building a critical access hospital.

Before we left town, Pam and her husband, Gary, threw an ice cream social party for us on a Sunday afternoon at their beautiful home, which was then blossoming in flowers all around. This was a gathering of friends, most of whom we had met during our district days. Jim and Ingrid presented us with a beautiful wood-and-iron bench, plus a rocker on which Ingrid had painted personal and beautiful scenes of Pagosa including the stunning mountains we had hiked, skied and loved. With amazing craftsmanship, Ingrid

Detail of the bench created by Ingrid Knoll.

had carefully worked in the names of our friends. The art work was gorgeous, and the hours of toil it must have taken were evident by the intricacy of the paintings. We were honored and overwhelmed. This was a heartfelt and beautiful ending to our time in Pagosa.

In reviewing the past year, I saw that though it had been a difficult time, in the end success had reigned. The community appeared satisfied that the district was now on the right path. In the "old" days large and angry crowds had attended board meetings, but now virtually only the board and committee members showed up for these meetings. I almost missed the ribald days with the "old" Board—well, not really.

All in all, I know that I contributed to this success, weathering that first year, helping to get our slate elected, and in the second year pushing for the critical access hospital. Intermixed were failures: not being able to accomplish the merger of our public clinic with that of Dr. Pruitt's Family Medicine and the closing of our clinic. However, I believe that these were learning experiences which we had to go through and from which we benefited.

This was my first involvement in politics, and I am pretty sure my last. Although I had many stressful times and disappointments during these two plus years, I also had many joys and successes. I enjoyed the passion of the moment. I'll always cherish my time in Pagosa, a truly beautiful mountain town, and my time on the health district board. Both are great memories. Lastly, working with our guru, General Jim; this foot soldier appreciated his leadership, our camaraderie, our many strategizing DQ lunches, and, of course, our lasting friendship.

This volunteer work without financial remuneration was as satisfying as any work I had done as a physician. The void left by my retirement from practicing medicine was more than filled by this unique experience.

EPILOGUE

Sitting in my office, now two years since I started writing this tale, I am looking down on the winding Columbia River. It is a misty morning with gray, water-laden clouds hanging over the valley, ready to unburden themselves onto the patchwork fields and trees below. When we moved to the Pacific Northwest, I had feared that the long rainy season here would have a depressing effect on me. Patti looks on days like this as cozy, a time to stay inside, curl up and read a book. I, too, now find these soft, rainy days as snug times for sitting by the fire for reading, writing, and recalling a memory or two.

A highlight occurred last year when our board chair, Pam Hopkins, called to ask if I would participate in the ground-breaking ceremony planned for the new critical access hospital. A team of wild horses couldn't have kept me away.

A crowd of several hundred people witnessed the ground breaking. Wearing a white hard hat and using a gold-painted shovel, I joined the present board members in tossing a spade full of dirt into the air to the clicking of numerous cameras. For me it was a very meaningful ceremony, a physical confirmation of our success.

Groundbreaking! From left, Bob Goodman, Michelle Wisel, Bob Scott, Pam Hopkins, Neal Townsend, Kitzel Farrah, DVM, Jim Pruitt, M.D., and Dick Blide, M.D.

This occasion made the front page of the *Pagosa Springs Sun*[19] with an accompanying picture of the ceremony and a glowing article. One of the prominent citizens in Pagosa came up to me after the ceremony and thanked me for my efforts on behalf of the health district and the community. I was touched by her kindness.

After consulting with architects, builders, and financiers, the board had decided to build a critical access hospital of some 35,000 square feet. Several architectural plans were submitted to the board, with the selection chosen interestingly looking similar to the CAH built in Del Norte, Colorado, as is described in this story. Because the Dr. Mary Fisher Medical Center (clinic) had been so well built back in 1996 and planned for expansion, the hospital was built on the same site and incorporated the clinic building into the architectural plan.

Gary Hopkins, Joy Sinnott, Patti Blide, Dick Blide, M.D., and Pam Hopkins

The board of directors largely met their financial goals for the CAH, helped by the fact that in the past year they had raised over a million dollars in donations. Four prominent families in the area offered to donate $500,000 if the community would match this figure. This happened with board members alone donating more than 20 percent of this amount, which assured the community that the board was 100 percent committed to the critical access hospital. The district also applied for the State of Colorado Mineral and Energy Grant for $500,000, which was approved. This was the grant for which I had prematurely wanted to submit an application. The bulk of the building funds are coming from a twelve-million-dollar loan. To obtain the lowest possible interest rate on this loan, they are using as collateral the mil levy mandated by taxes due the district. This was proposed as a bond issue at the election in May 2006, and it passed by an overwhelming majority, a

13-to-one margin. Just recently a bank came forward to carry this loan. Most recently, Pam Hopkins and new board member, Michelle Visel, submitted a grant to Caring for Colorado for $200,000 to buy a used CT scanner that Mercy Hospital was putting up for sale. This grant was approved, the largest grant ever made by this charitable organization.

The board members whose terms were expiring all ran for re-election in May 2006. All were returned to office. Surprisingly, or maybe not, they had no opposition. I believe this was a sincere gesture of confidence and appreciation by the community for a job well done by the board of directors of the Upper San Juan Health Service District.

In September chairwoman Pam retired from this position, and vice-chair Neil Townsend took over the helm. Pam remains a board director. The editor of the *Pagosa Springs Sun*, Karl Isberg, wrote a glowing editorial on the great job that Pam Hopkins had done as chairwoman, particularly her selfless devotion to the job without letting petty politics get in the way. He pointed out that the health district board had changed from one of rancor to where it was now a model that other public agencies would do well to replicate.[20]

The new district manager provided by Mercy Hospital improved the billing and collection service and procedures that were still in a deplorable state in the spring of 2005. By the summer of 2005 the district's finances finally reverted to the black with all loans repaid, a rarity for the district in its 20-year history. The district manager's contract was not renewed because he eventually did spend more time on his primary job at Mercy and less on the business matters in Pagosa. Fortunately, a new retiree to Pagosa with good business acumen, Pat Haney, volunteered to be the interim district manager. Then, in late 2007 the board, after considerable soul searching, chose a CEO with an excellent background in hospital administration.

Dr. Jim Pruitt and his Family Medicine Clinic lost Dr. Picarro, who moved his practice to Durango. They then added two new physicians to their staff and are as busy as ever.

The EMS, for a while remaining under the part-time direction of Joy and Brian Sinnott, grew and flourished. A new EMS ops manager has been hired, one with good credentials and finally at a salary commensurate with the position. EMS continues to have strong ties with the Mercy Hospital Emergency Department, which we instituted in the summer of 2005, Mercy providing the medical advisor, supervising training of the EMT's, and having jurisdiction over ambulance calls. These are all goals we had envisioned three years back in 2003.

There is now a close working relationship with Mercy Hospital, which was also one of the major goals of Guru Jim's Position Statement of 2003. All of the other goals have been met as well. The one change that stands out, in stark contrast to the past, is that the local physicians have been made to feel that they are now a part of the health service district. Dr. Jim Pruitt continues his position as a board director.

The frosting on the cake was the opening of the critical access hospital, ahead of schedule, on January 7, 2008, with the name: The Pagosa Mountain Hospital.

I, too, believe that the Upper San Juan Health Service District can now serve as a model for other organizations in Pagosa Springs and for other communities, as Karl Isgard, editor of the *Pagosa Springs Sun* newspaper said in one of his editorials. It demonstrated what can be accomplished in a small, rural town in America, first by planning with vision and then by the community carefully

Pagosa Mountain Hospital, the new critical access hospital.

choosing
dedicated,
hard-working
personnel to fill
board positions.
Medical
personnel must
be included on
a health service
board because

without them, direction is likely to be misguided, as demonstrated in the telling of this story. The addition of committees of experts to advise the board is important. The finance committee in this story was vital to the restoration of fiscal integrity to the district. Lastly and importantly, a community needs to remain vigilant, aware of the actions of their public representatives in order to remedy a bad situation as soon as possible through the election process or by legal means if necessary. Rural communities are more prone to political intrigue because there are fewer checks and balances than in urban areas, due to limited population and diversity. What happened in this small rural mountain town could occur again anywhere in America.

This tale demonstrates that it is important to be in contact with your contemporaries in surrounding areas, to get their input, to see what they are doing, and to measure your progress and success by their growth.

Jim stated in the beginning that chaos begets change, which proved to be true in this case. In fact, I feel that the changes that we achieved would not have occurred had it not been for the chaotic events that occurred at the beginning of this story that virtually mandated a change. The community awoke to the challenge and made it happen.

The new hospital's helipad
is ready for emergencies.

With the passage of time, we can more easily evaluate the

events of the past. I can see three occurrences that predominated in the health care successes in this town. First was the vision of Dr. Jim Knoll in being able to appraise the early chaotic problem accurately and to come up with a plan that ultimately proved to be successful.

Secondly, I believe we picked up the baton from Norm Vance and his community group such that together we slogged through the trenches, baton held high, to motivate and maintain the building momentum in the community until election time when a change was overwhelmingly mandated.

Thirdly, the persons selected to be the new board of directors and committee members could not have been better chosen, as demonstrated by what they accomplished and are still attaining, their vision and effort culminating in a critical access hospital, a first for the area.

I feel fortunate to have been a part of this team effort, a truly once-in-a-lifetime

H♥ARTFELT

experience.

A SUMMARY COMMENT

BAD BOARD, GOOD BOARD

My time on the board of the USJHSD covered both the worst and the best in board governance within a public organization, giving me a first-hand perspective of both sides of the governance equation.

I have extracted from this story what I believe to be relevant facts and have indicated in a narrative fashion what could have been done to correct and to avoid bad situations. This may be of benefit to other organizations having similar problems.

Disruptive situations: When I first joined the health district as a board member, I soon became aware that the district manager (DM) was the focus of a controversy. As we saw, this conflict centered about the firing of employees and the harassment of employees so that they would quit. The intent was to create a new staff wholly beholden to the DM. Initially, the DM did not have control of the board, but she soon discovered that she could actually do as she pleased without fear of reprimand because no one on the board knew how to handle a disruptive administrator nor did they openly question her actions.

The board and administration eventually heeded the advice of several townspeople to bring in an independent person to intercede and mediate a solution to the employee problem. The mediator selected made recommendations after only a cursory examination of the problem and before any mediation had taken place. She erred by recommending that the chairman of the board resign because he was a part of the problem. This was true from the standpoint that he had not done anything to solve the problem, but he was not the cause of the conflict; the DM was the instigator. The mediator was hired by the DM and not by the board. By such action it could be presumed the mediator was biased in the DM's direction, for the mediator offered no criticism of the DM in her initial and only report.

This mediator's error begat a second mistake, which was the chairman accepting her recommendation and abdicating his responsibility as a board member and as chairman. It was obvious that the conflict was between the DM and the employees. The chairman had it within his power, with the board's approval, to reprimand the DM and bring an end to the employee dilemma. He, better than anyone else, had to know that his leaving would exacerbate, not improve, the situation. The chairman had shown strong leadership in the prior several years when he had led the district out of a horrible mess due to past poor leadership and financial shenanigans. But now, for some unknown reason, the chairman could not bring himself to buck the DM. Perhaps this was because he had been instrumental in choosing her as the DM and was now not willing to admit that this had been a mistake. So, both the mediator and chairman were mistaken in their decisions.

Another obvious solution would have been to set up an independent *ad hoc* committee to review employee complaints, firings, etc., and to make corrective recommendations to the board. A personnel policy was in place at the time, but it was controlled by the administration and so was of no use to the employees. It did not include an appeals policy, as it should have, to a group outside the administration.

This resignation by the chairman gave the administrator the chance to bring in her own chairman and shortly thereafter another board member, both chosen because they acquiesced to the DM's lead. Thereafter any dissension was ineffective because the DM had absolute control of the majority of the board. It then took a year, until the next election, for the townspeople to correct a situation that could have been prevented in the first place. A weak and ineffective board had allowed this to happen and, to boot, when things became difficult, board members resigned rather than tackle the problem. This left the employees to fend for themselves. A strong and knowledgeable board is essential for good governance.

What could have been done at that time to affect a better outcome? A mediator with more experience would have delved more deeply into the problem before making any recommendations and then should have worked with the board, not the administrator, in trying to resolve the situation. If there is a major problem threatening an organization, one does not seek a solution through a middleman. One starts at the top.

The inexperienced mediator allowed herself to be manipulated. Though she was forced to bring in an outsider, the DM was wily enough to take advantage of this situation and maneuver the chairman out of the picture via the mediator. Once this was done, the DM dropped the mediator and her "healing circles." The DM had outwitted the board. There were good people on the board, but no one stepped forward to take charge and lead the district out of this debacle.

This would have been the perfect time for the board to bring in someone expert in the functioning of boards and administrations, such as a parliamentarian like Ron Clodfelter, who served us well in this position at a later date when the new board took charge. I have no doubt that Clodfelter would have clearly seen the problem and would have laid out a plan for the board, and not the administration, to solve this dilemma. If governance is a problem, bringing in a parliamentarian is a good solution.

Another answer: as we saw, when the new board was in place, a committee of experts, such as a Rules and By-laws Committee, would have supported the board and would have likely forestalled the untoward events that occurred. I believe that the establishment and the use of committees by boards is an invaluable tool, as was so well demonstrated by the help they afforded the new board in this story. The old board did have committees but they were ineffectual, in no small measure because the board did not use them. Also, a weak board is not likely to birth strong committees.

The importance of vision: recapitulating, the old board came up with a vision for the future in the fall of 2003. However, they were handicapped by their past. They were not trusted by the two groups that they needed to work with to make progress, the local physicians and the Mercy Hospital group in Durango. Because of their past bad experiences with the district, these groups refused any association with the district until a change in leadership occurred. A good dose of foresight on the part of those in control of the district at that time could have avoided this problem and the cascading of negative events that followed.

Next, the Jim Knoll Position Statement outlined a vision for the future for the new board, correcting the deficiencies in the health care system at the time. Amazingly, the new board was able to accomplish all six of these recommendations within a year of their taking office.

Then a new vision was needed. There should always be a goal toward which one is working. Maintaining the status quo is not enough. If one is not progressing, one is probably regressing simply because others will not be standing still. During the new board's year of climbing out of a mountain of debt, they were able to turn an unfortunate situation into a golden opportunity and a new vision. Medicare told this board that they had been mistakenly reimbursing us for ambulance trips to our local clinic facilities and that they would be stopping this practice. Our then-district manager, Allan Hughes, alertly recognized that only by having a critical access hospital (CAH) could we recoup this loss. This, then, became our new vision and triggered the successive steps that would lead to actually having a CAH by early 2008. In so doing, Pagosa Springs was finally able to take advantage of and benefit from one of the federal programs established to help small rural communities.

Always have a vision: I am no longer a member of this community or of the board of directors of the Upper San Juan Health Service District, but I would remind those still involved of the value of using the federally-mandated program to help small rural committees: a rural health clinic. Sooner or later such an entity would be of benefit to the area in providing better care for the poor and indigent as well as providing improved benefits for the physicians involved. Boards should always be aware of and take advantage of federal, state and private programs that provide funds and grant money for their development, as was so well exemplified in this story and taken advantage of by the new board.

How do you choose good executives? I talked to our first board chairman, Dick Babillis, on one occasion, about how they chose their DM back in 2002. They advertised the position in a multi-state area and received a good assortment of candidates. They requested references which they perused. Those candidates who appeared to best satisfy their requirements for the position were then interviewed. To this point one would say that they followed standard procedure. I mentioned before that the old district's DM could be very ingratiating when she so desired, so I am sure that she presented a good interview. It was also mentioned that she had submitted references, particularly from some of the physicians who had worked in the student health clinic part-time. So it was no surprise to me that Eve was chosen for the position.

Should there have been any further investigation? At least one more step should have been taken. When a person is looking for a new position, they are unlikely to name their employer as a reference for fear of jeopardizing their present position. However, when one is told that he or she has the job except for one last reference, one would be expected to accede to the request for a reference from his or her employer. As we saw from the personnel record received from Texas Tech University, a reference from this source might not have been accepted as favorable. This one last step should have been taken.

There are two further steps that have come into being in recent years. A detailed search on the Internet for criminal activity, bankruptcy, etc., is easily done. Also, checking records, such as verifying college degrees and work records, is more common these days. However, there is no procedure that is going to be 100 percent infallible.

Could a board be too strong? I mentioned previously that our new board was quite strong, each member having expertise in different areas, but primarily in the areas of health care and business. We all worked well together, and no one tried to dominate the scene. We had equality and mutual respect even when there was some disagreement. We had unity too in that we all thought so much alike, but equality was foremost.

Because we were all new to board governance, some things were learned through experience. Not knowing better, we broke the rule of Boards set policy; Administrations implement policy. In our rush to get our new policies moving in the right direction as soon as possible, we all deluged our district manager with suggestions and recommendations, and even worse, these varied from one board member to another. Our DM indicated that at times he worked 70 hours a week. More than halfway through the year he indicated that he didn't know what to do. He couldn't make everyone happy. We finally recognized this problem and subsequently funneled all our suggestions through the chairman, who filtered the information and made recommendations to the DM from this single source. However, by then the damage had already been done. Considering the circumstances, I felt that our DM had done a very good job. He had successfully implemented our policy for getting out of debt. We would now have to be more careful in how we related to a new district manager in the future, respecting his or her turf, making clear the board's duties versus those of the administration, and making clear the demarcation between the two. This is all made very clear in John Carver's book, *Boards That Make a Difference: A New Design for Leadership in Nonprofit and Public Organizatons*.[21] It would have behooved us to have read this book before we took office. It would have helped us avoid this problem. It is my opinion that this or similar books should be required reading for new and prospective board directors.

SUMMARY

This chapter has taken the untoward events that occurred in a public organization over a four-year period and has indicated how these problems could have been avoided, or once present, how they could have been more readily corrected. With vigilance, a community and its public organizations should be able to avoid these problematic situations.

Volunteer work on boards, committees and elsewhere can be most rewarding. It can also be difficult and require resolve and perseverance which in the end, with success, can be even more rewarding. If one wants to give back to society for the benefits received in life, there can be no better way than through volunteer work of some kind.

NOTES

Book 1, Chapter 1

1. Tess Noel Baker, "Public Rancor Follows Health Chief's Stance," *The Pagosa Springs Sun*, 9/18/03.
2. Baker, "Director Admits Erring with Email," *The Pagosa Springs Sun*, 3/06/03.
3. Baker, "Consultant's Report Cites Morale, Management Ills," *The Pagosa Springs Sun*, 2/20/03.
4. Baker, "Health District Board Chairman Resigns," *The Pagosa Springs Sun*, 2/20/03.

Chapter 2

5. Baker, "Health Board Agrees to Open Negotiations," *The Pagosa Springs Sun*, 4/17/03.

Chapter 4

6. Baker, "Six Point Plan Advanced," *The Pagosa Springs Sun*, 5/08/03.
7. Baker, "Health District's Financial Turnaround Cited," *The Pagosa Springs Sun*, 6/19/03.
8. Baker, "Two Errors Void Health Board Recall Petitions," *The Pagosa Springs Sun*, 6/26/03.

Chapter 5

9. Karl Isberg, "Hope Springs Eternal," Editorial, *The Pagosa Springs Sun*, 7/24/03.

Chapter 7

10. David L. Weiner, *Power Freaks: Dealing with Them in the Workplace or Anyplace* (New York, Prometheus Books, 2002), 22.

Chapter 9

11. Baker, "Public Rancor Follows Health Chief's Stance," *The Pagosa Springs Sun*, 9/18/03.
12. Edward Mendelson, *The Things That Matter* (New York, Pantheon Books, 2006), 83.

13. Karl Isberg, "Make a Change," Editorial, *The Pagosa Springs Sun*, 9/18/03.

Chapter 18

14. Webster's New World, *Robert's Rules of Order* (Indianapolis, Wiley Publishing, 2001), 187.
15. Dick Babillis, Letters-to-the-Editor, *The Pagosa Springs Sun*, 1/15/04, 43.

Chapter 21

16. Tom Carosello, "DEA Procedure Flap Keys Health Panel Turmoil," *The Pagosa Springs Sun*, 4/15/04.
17. Carosello, "Ads Backing Health District Administrator Irk Employees," *The Pagosa Springs Sun*, 4/15/04.

Book 2, Chapter 15

18. Robert Jaworski, *Synchronicity: The Inner Path of Leadership* (San Francisco, Berrett-Koehler, 1998)

Chapter 20

19. Chuck McGuire, "District Breaks Ground, Hopkins Resigns," *The Pagosa Springs Sun*, 9/07/06.
20. Karl Isberg, "Successful Leadership," Editorial, *The Pagosa Springs Sun*, 9/14/06.

Chapter 21

21. John Carver, *Boards That Make a Difference: A New Design for Leadership in Non-profit and Public Organizations* (San Francisco, Jossey-Bass Publications, 1997).

Richard W. Blide, M.D., one of four children, was born in Rochester, New York, during the depression. He graduated from the University of Rochester and then followed his interest in medicine with a medical degree from Albany Medical College.

After serving two years in the U.S. Public Health Service, Dr. Blide took a residency in internal medicine, followed by a fellowship in pulmonary medicine at the University of Maryland Medical Center in Baltimore, Maryland. He joined the faculty there as a professor of medicine, practiced academic medicine, and established the first pulmonary laboratory in the chest service, which he ran for seven years.

He had a broad and varied career thereafter, first being medical director of the Will Rogers Hospital, a general chest disease hospital, in Saranac Lake, New York, for six years. He subsequently moved to Dallas, Texas, where he switched careers and practiced preventive medicine at the Cooper Clinic. There, he met and married his wife, Patti. Lastly, he practiced physical medicine and rehabilitation in Dallas and Lubbock, Texas, until his retirement in 1999.

Heartfelt, a memoir, speaks of his years in retirement in Pagosa Springs, Colorado, where he and Patti enjoyed mountain hiking and skiing along with four-wheel off-road excursions. His many hours of work on the board of the Upper San Juan Health Service District serve as the basis of this story.

Dr. Blide and Patti presently reside in rural Washington State, where they enjoy hiking, water sports, and writing.